The Developing Child

Recent decades have witnessed unprecedented advances in research on human development. In those same decades there have been profound changes in public policy toward children. Each book in the Developing Child series reflects the importance of such research in its own right and as it bears on the formulation of policy. It is the purpose of the series to make the findings of this research available to those who are responsible for raising a new generation and for shaping policy in its behalf. We hope that these books will provide rich and useful information for parents, educators, child-care professionals, students of developmental psychology, and all others concerned with the challenge of human growth.

Jerome Bruner
New York University
Michael Cole
University of California, San Diego
Annette Karmiloff-Smith
Medical Research Council, London
SERIES EDITORS

THE DEVELOPING CHILD SERIES

The
Caring Child

Nancy Eisenberg

Harvard University Press
Cambridge, Massachusetts
London, England   1992

This book is printed on acid-free paper, and its binding materials
have been chosen for strength and durability.

Library of Congress Cataloging-in-Publication Data

Eisenberg, Nancy.
    The caring child / Nancy Eisenberg.
      p.   cm.—(The Developing child)
    Includes bibliographical references and index.
    ISBN 0-674-09725-4 (alk. paper).—ISBN 0-674-09726-2 (pbk.:
alk. paper)
      1. Helping behavior in children.   2. Altruism in children.   I. Title.
II. Series.
    BF723.H45E56   1992
    155.4'18232—dc20
    91-15214
        CIP

The
Caring Child

Nancy Eisenberg

Harvard University Press
Cambridge, Massachusetts
London, England   1992

This book is printed on acid-free paper, and its binding materials
have been chosen for strength and durability.

Library of Congress Cataloging-in-Publication Data

Eisenberg, Nancy.
  The caring child / Nancy Eisenberg.
    p. cm.—(The Developing child)
  Includes bibliographical references and index.
  ISBN 0-674-09725-4 (alk. paper).—ISBN 0-674-09726-2 (pbk.:
alk. paper)
    1. Helping behavior in children. 2. Altruism in children. I. Title.
II. Series.
  BF723.H45E56 1992
  155.4'18232—dc20
  91-15214
    CIP

Acknowledgments

This book reflects the support of many people and organizations. Time and support for research were provided by grants from the National Science Foundation and the National Institute of Child Health and Development. Some of the research reported in this book was supported by previous grants from these organizations, as well as the National Institute of Mental Health and the Foundation for Child Development. Over the years, numerous people have contributed to my thinking about the development of prosocial behavior and empathy. These include Joseph Campos, Robert Cialdini, Richard Fabes, Martin Hoffman, Marian Radke-Yarrow, Carolyn Zahn-Waxler, and especially Paul Mussen. I am also indebted to Jerry Harris and George Knight, who read earlier versions of some chapters. Finally, I appreciate the support of my husband, Jerry.

Contents

The Caring Child

1/ The Study of Prosocial Behavior

Everyone helps, comforts, and shares with others at some time or another. But not all people assist to the same degree and for the same reasons. Consider the following examples of the sharing behavior of three preschool girls—Erin, Heather, and Lauren—in a daycare setting.

Erin was sitting at a table with other children, playing with Play-Doh. Jonathan came to the table and looked around for Play-Doh and utensils to use. When he saw that all the Play-Doh was in use, Jonathan started to display facial cues of distress. Erin looked up at Jonathan, pinched off a piece off her Play-Doh, smiled, and gave it to him, saying, "Here's some you can play with."

Heather was sitting at the table kneading Play-Doh when Mark approached and looked for some to use but found none available. When Mark initially showed signs of being upset, Heather looked at him but did nothing. Then Mark turned to Heather and said, "Can I have some?" Without any verbal response or display of emotion, Heather tore off a piece of Play-Doh and handed it to Mark.

Lauren was playing with Play-Doh when Eric approached, searched for some but found none, exhibited mild distress, and asked Lauren for some of hers. Instead of giving him some, she simply said, "No," and moved the Play-Doh closer to her. Then Eric said, "If you give me some, I'll give you some of my candy." Lauren then tore off a small piece of Play-Doh and gave it to Eric as he handed her a piece of his candy.

All three of the girls described in these incidents ultimately shared Play-Doh with a peer. Yet the nature or the quality of their sharing behavior appeared to differ in fundamental ways. Erin shared without being asked and with a display of goodwill, perhaps in response to her recognition that Jonathan was unhappy. Heather did not share until asked but passively complied with Mark's request once he directly asked her for some Play-Doh. Finally, Lauren refused to share her Play-Doh with Eric until he offered her something in exchange for doing so.

Although we cannot know with certainty why each of the three girls shared, it seems likely that their motives for doing so were quite different. Among other reasons, Erin may have assisted because she felt sorry for Jonathan, because she had been taught that sharing was a desirable behavior, or simply because she was sociable and liked Jonathan's company. Heather, who shared only after being asked directly for the Play-Doh, probably did not want to share but may have felt it was easier to comply with Mark's request than to deal with his reaction if she refused to give him some. Another possibility was that she was too shy or inhibited to offer Mark Play-Doh until he asked for some. Finally, Lauren did not seem to be concerned at all by Eric's distress; rather, her sharing appeared to be motivated solely by self-interest.

If Erin's, Heather's, and Lauren's reactions were typical for each girl, why did they behave so differently, and how might they differ from children who seldom share or help under any circumstances? Was the disparity in their reactions a result of differences in how much they valued sharing, in their social competence and ability to assert themselves (for example, in the ability to refuse a request), in the degree to which they could understand the feelings of the boy without Play-Doh, or some combination of these or other factors? Were the differences in behavior learned at home or in other settings such a school, or did they reflect some aspect of personality that is inherited? Finally, would it be possible to alter the ways in which the three girls interact with people who are in need or distress?

Such questions, concerning *prosocial behavior* and its development, are the focus of this book. Prosocial behavior frequently is defined as voluntary behavior intended to benefit another, such as helping, sharing, and comforting behaviors. Psychologists consider many prosocial behaviors to be motivated by factors such as the expectation of concrete rewards, social approval, or the desire to reduce one's own negative internal states (for example, guilt or distress from observing a needy other). But prosocial behaviors also include *altruistic behaviors*—that is, prosocial behaviors that are motivated by sympathy for others or by the desire to adhere to internalized moral principles. Psychologists generally consider altruistic behaviors to be more moral than are prosocial behaviors motivated by factors such as the desire to avoid punishment or to obtain rewards or social approval. Thus, altruism is of special interest to developmental psychologists, educators, and other people who work with children.

Altruistic behaviors, then, are performed for different reasons from some other prosocial behaviors. Thus, an understanding of people's *motives* for assisting others is important for understanding altruism and its development. Only by understanding the motivations behind people's prosocial behaviors, and how these motives develop and are elicited in various situations, can we begin to promote systematically the development of kindness and caring.

A HISTORICAL PERSPECTIVE

Given the importance of understanding human kindness, our knowledge of prosocial behavior is surprisingly limited. One reason, of course, is the complexity of human behavior and of the motivations for it. Human behavior is determined by many factors, and it is very difficult to study how all these interact.

Another reason is that social scientists and educators have begun to study prosocial behavior only relatively recently. Although philosophers such as David Hume were interested in sympathy and prosocial behavior centuries ago,[1] before 1970 most psychologists and educators were studying aggression and other negative behaviors, not prosocial behavior.

Social scientists, like other people, tend to focused on issues that are salient and are seen as a potential threat to themselves or to society. Since violence, stealing, and dishonesty have highly visible negative outcomes, it is not surprising that researchers focused on understanding and alleviating these negative behaviors—behaviors that threaten the functioning of society. After 1945, there was also considerable interest in understanding how people could have committed the atrocities that were commonplace during the Second World War. Researchers focused on the factors that promoted prejudice, blind obedience to authority, and the emotional numbness that enabled people to kill civilians and children en masse.[2]

Interest in altruism and humanitarian practices burgeoned in the 1960s, when the civil rights movement and the Vietnam War caused many Americans to question their values, to protest against what was perceived as an unjust war, and to demand an end to discriminatory policies toward minorities and the poor. A particularly dramatic incident also helped to stimulate thinking and research on helping behavior. In 1964 a young woman, Kitty Genovese, was brutally murdered near her apartment building in Queens, New York. Witnesses to the event did nothing to help her. No one even called the police until after Genovese was dead. The publicity surrounding this incident shocked the public with the realization that people can be totally apathetic in emergencies, and roused psychologists to try to determine why people help, or do not help, those in distress.[3] The surge of interest in prosocial behavior has continued unabated ever since.[4]

OVERVIEW

This book surveys what is known about the emergence of prosocial behaviors early in life, factors that affect the development of prosocial behavior, and individual differences in behaviors such as helping, sharing, and comforting. When do children first exhibit prosocial behavior, particularly altruism? How do helping, sharing, and comforting behaviors change with age? Why are some children more prosocial than others? Do these differences in prosocial behavior arise from nature, from nurture, or from both? Can prosocial tendencies be enhanced by parents' and educators' deliberate attempts to instill altruistic motives and teach prosocial behaviors? The following chapters address these and related questions.

However, the answers to these questions are rarely simple. Prosocial behavior, like any other social behavior, is frequently determined by a variety of factors. Thus, although we know about some of the factors that appear to affect prosocial development, there are no simple recipes for raising a prosocial child. Much more remains to be learned, and each new bit of information raises new questions.

One final word is needed. The focus of this book is the *development* of prosocial behavior in children. Thus, I do not discuss much of the large body of literature concerning adults' prosocial behavior.[5] Much of the adult literature concerns factors in the immediate context that affect whether or not someone helps or shares rather than why some adults are more prosocial than others.[6] In contrast, the primary focus here is the origins of prosocial behavior and how it can be enhanced—a focus that reflects the belief that we as parents, teachers, or members of society can promote a cooperative and caring orientation in our children.

2/ Benevolent Babies and Caring Children

For a long time most philosophers and psychologists—as well as many laypeople—considered infants, toddlers, and young children to be very self-interested and amoral. This view was reinforced by Sigmund Freud's assertion that infants are born possessing only the id (the structure of personality concerned with innate, instinctual, irrational impulses and self-gratification) and do not develop a superego, which contains the conscience, until 4 to 6 years of age. The idea that young children are concerned only with their own needs was perpetuated by the writings of the noted psychologist Jean Piaget, who asserted that children were unable to understand others' perspectives until they were 6 or 7 years old.[1] If children cannot understand another's point of view, why would they be motivated to assist others?

It is now clear that children not only have a rudimentary understanding of others' perspectives in the first few years of life but also are capable of other-oriented, prosocial behavior.[2] Indeed, even 1-to 2-year-olds sometimes exhibit what appears to be altruistic behavior. However, the nature of prosocial responding does seem to change somewhat during the first few years of life.

THE FIRST THREE YEARS

The seeds of prosocial development may be present even in the first year of life. Neonates tend to cry in response to the crying of another baby. Some researchers believe that such crying may be a precursor of early empathic responding.[3] However, there are other possible explanations, and it is unlikely that this reflexive crying is a prosocial, other-oriented response. Young infants may simply confuse another infant's crying with their own. In fact 6-month-olds seldom respond with distress to peers' distresses.

Nonetheless, even 6-month-olds sometimes exhibit interest in others' distresses; for example, 49 percent of the infants in one study responded to distressed peers with actions such as leaning toward, gesturing toward, touching, or otherwise contacting the peer.[4] However, whether infants respond in this way as a result of concern or mere curiosity is unclear.

RESPONDING TO OTHERS' DISTRESS

By 10 to 14 months of age, infants frequently become agitated and disturbed when they view others in distress. They may attend in tense silence, whimper, or cry like the 11- and 14-month-olds in the following two examples:

Sari [an 11-month-old] (on witnessing physical pain) looked sad, puckered up, and burst out crying. She continued to cry intensely. She crawled over to her mother to be picked up.

Jenny [a 14-month-old] observed a crying 6-month-old baby. She watched; tears welled in her eyes; she began to cry.[5]

In such instances it is not clear whether infants are truly concerned about the other person or whether the other person's distress merely upsets them. The fact that very young children such as the 11-month-old described above often seek comfort for themselves when exposed to others' distress supports the latter explanation. Indeed, Martin Hoffman has argued that children in the first year of life do not clearly differentiate between self and other, and therefore are unclear as to who is experiencing any distress they witness.[6]

At about 1 year of age, children's reactions to others in distress start to change. Becoming distressed oneself in response to the distress of others decreases in relative frequency during the second year of life.[7] In addition, at about 1 year children begin to exhibit reactions that suggest they understand that their own distresses and others' are not one and the same. For example, Hoffman described one child

> whose typical response to both his own and another's distress, beginning late in the first year, was to suck his thumb with one hand and pull his ear with the other . . . Something new happened at 12 months. On seeing a sad look on his father's face, he proceeded to look sad and suck his thumb, while pulling on his father's ear— as though he was just beginning to recognize the difference between self-in-distress and other-in-distress but the distinction was not yet clear.[8]

Similarly, Carolyn Zahn-Waxler, Marian Radke-Yarrow, and Robert King observed a 12-month-old who, when confronted with another person in distress, alternated between gently touching the victim and touching himself.[9]

In the second year of life, children sometimes make focused efforts to interact positively with others in distress. Often these efforts initially include positive physical contact such as patting or touching. By 18 to 24 months of age, the interventions include more con-

trolled and positive actions directed toward the victim.
Consider the following examples:

> A neighbor's baby cries. Jenny [18 months old] looked
> startled, her body stiffened. She approached and tried
> to give the baby cookies. She followed him around and
> began to whimper herself. She then tried to stroke his
> hair, but he pulled away. Later, she approached her
> mother, led her to the baby, and tried to put mother's
> hand on the baby's head. He calmed down a little, but
> Jenny still looked worried. She continued to bring him
> toys and to pat his head and shoulders.[10]

> C [a 21-month-old] is playing a game of jumping off
> chair arm to cushion on the floor. She jumps and with
> her shoe accidentally hits sibling, who cries. M comforts
> sibling. C comes to sibling with concerned expression,
> strokes her head.[11]

> The 15-month-old, Len, was a stocky boy with a fine
> round tummy, and he played at this time a particular
> game with his parents which always made him laugh.
> His game was to come towards them, walking in an odd
> way, pulling up his T-shirt and showing his big stom-
> ach. One day his elder brother fell off the climbing frame
> in the garden and cried vigorously. Len watched sol-
> emnly. Then he approached his brother, pulling up his
> T-shirt and showing his tummy, vocalizing, and looking
> at his brother.[12]

Reactions such as these have been found to increase
significantly in frequency at about 18 months of age.[13]

Hoffman has described the 1-to-2-year-old as experiencing "egocentric" empathy. In his view,

> the child is fully aware of the self and other as distinct
> physical entities and thus [is] able for the first time to
> experience empathic distress while also being aware that
> another person, and not the self, is the victim. Children

cannot yet fully distinguish between their own and other person's inner states, however, and are apt to confuse them with their own, as illustrated by their efforts to help others, which consist chiefly [in] giving the other person what they themselves find most comforting. Examples are a 13-month-old who responded with a distressed look to an adult who looked sad and then offered the adult his beloved doll; and another who ran to fetch his own mother to comfort a crying friend, even though the friend's mother was equally available.[14]

Children later in their second year tend to help or comfort other people more than younger children do, not only when they merely observe others in distress but also when they have caused the other person's distress. However, 2-year-olds are more likely than younger children to behave aggressively toward those they have hurt.[15]

Of course, young children do not always respond to another's distress in a prosocial manner; indeed, prosocial behavior among 18-month-olds is relatively rare, even at home. Children aged 18 to 36 months often simply ignore their siblings' distress or need or merely watch them express their distress. In addition, young children often exacerbate the situation when they have upset their siblings.[16]

Similarly, young children more often ignore peers' distress than respond positively. In one study, 16-to-33-month-olds responded to a peer's distress in a play setting only 22 percent of the time. However, most of these responses were prosocial; the children attempted to mediate or intervene on the peer's behalf, consoled the peer, or offered relevant information to the teacher. As might be expected, the children responded to the distress of a friend three times more often than to that of someone who was not a friend.[17]

SHARING AND HELPING

Not all prosocial interactions among young children involve a response to a distressed person. Sharing of objects in social interactions not involving distress increases during the first year of life and is common among 1-to-2-year-olds.[18] Indeed, sharing of toys has been noted among children under 1 year of age:

> A few weeks ago I spent some time on the floor with our secretary's 11-month-old baby girl. When she picked up a toy, I held out my hand. After a pause she would give it to me. Then she picked up her favourite toy. When I held my hand out, she held it closer to herself, then smiled at me, reached with the other hand for another toy, and gave that to me.[19]

Such sharing by young children may not be motivated primarily by concern for the other person, however; giving and cooperative exchanges of objects seem to be effective ways for young children to sustain positive interchanges with others.[20]

Young children also frequently help (or try to help) with household chores. They readily help make beds, stack books, set tables, and sweep. For example, in studies of 18-, 24-, and 30-month-olds, Harriet Rheingold found that even 18-month-olds frequently participated in some everyday housekeeping tasks performed by adults, without being directed to do so. The children often assisted fathers and unfamiliar adults, as well as their mothers. Their behavior was goal-oriented and not aimless, and was not limited to imitation of adults' behaviors. Although it cannot be known if the children's goal was primarily to assist the adult, their behavior would be considered by many people as a positive social behavior.[21]

THE PRESCHOOL YEARS

Most parents and other adults believe that children become more helpful, caring, and generous as they move into the preschool years. There appears to be some truth to such beliefs, although some of the changes may be more in the minds of the adults than reflected in children's actual behavior.

RESPONDING TO OTHERS' DISTRESS

Children's comforting behaviors seem to increase in frequency from age 2 to age 3.[22] In addition, 3-year-olds' responses to others' distresses seem to be more appropriate and competent than those of 18-month-olds. This change in the quality of responding may reflect an increased ability to take another's perspective—to understand how other people think and feel. As Hoffman has argued:

> With the beginning of a role-taking capability, at about 2 or 3 years, children become aware that other people's feelings may sometimes differ from theirs, and their perspectives are based on their own needs and interpretation of events. More important, because children now know that the real world and their perceptions of it are not the same thing, and that the feelings of others are independent of their own, they become more responsive to cues about what the other is feeling.[23]

Because preschool children are better able than younger children to take the perspective of others, they are more motivated and better able to pinpoint the source of another's distress and to help in ways that are appropriate to the other's need. For example, an older child who observes another one crying will understand that the distressed child would prefer his or her own mother or teddy bear for comfort rather than the mother or bear of the observing child.

Although preschool children sometimes can and do respond to others in distress, comforting or distressed others is still relatively rare. Comforting behaviors are observed very infrequently in the preschool classroom, although children do occasionally approach an upset peer.[24] It is likely, however, that children are more prone to comfort family members than peers.

SHARING AND HELPING

In the preschool classroom sharing and helping behaviors are more frequent than comforting behaviors. Here are typical examples of such behaviors:

Lindsay was watching Sara construct a block building. As Sara ran low on blocks, Lindsay went to get her some.

Robert and Marc were talking as Robert started to put on an apron so he could paint. Marc helped Robert to tie the apron strings.

Amy and Dawn were coloring. Each had her own small pile of crayons. Amy asked for a red crayon, and Dawn passed her the red crayon in her pile.

Estimates of sharing behaviors per child in the classroom range from about 1 to 4 times per hour.[25] This wide range in part reflects differences in researchers' definitions of sharing.

Although Martin Hoffman believes that older preschoolers are likely to be better able than younger ones to discern another's desire for an object if the cues indicating the other person's wishes are subtle, it is not clear whether naturally occurring sharing behaviors increase with age during the preschool years.[26] Similarly, although preschoolers frequently help each other with tasks such as tying on aprons or fetching toys, it is not yet clear that such behavior increases in frequency during the preschool years.[27]

As one might expect, preschool children direct more prosocial behaviors toward some people than toward others. In the preschool classroom, much of children's prosocial behavior is directed toward the few children with whom they play most, and children tend to share with and help those children who share with and help them.[28] Thus, young children, like adults, are discriminating about whom they assist.

THE SCHOOL YEARS

RESPONDING TO OTHERS' DISTRESS

School-age children typically spend more time with their peers than do younger children and start to develop more intimate friendships. Thus, it is not surprising that there seems to be some increase in children's efforts to support and comfort one another in the elementary school years. For example, school children report that the amount of emotional support provided by friends increases from second to fourth grade.[29]

School-age children also may be more sensitive than younger ones to the needs of others in a variety of situations. For example, when confronted with a crying infant and its mother, an older child appears to be more likely to assist the crying infant and its mother physically and verbally, saying things such as "poor baby" and fetching a bottle and feeding the baby. Adolescents are even more likely than elementary school children to respond to an infant's birds for attention and to approach the baby; younger children tend to respond from a distance (smile, look, show the infant something, talk, make funny faces). Thus, older adolescents' responding to babies seems to be more contingent and appropriate than that of younger children.[30]

Not surprisingly, the ability to use language to comfort people increases substantially from childhood through adolescence. Older children are more likely than younger children to take the perspective of the distressed people when attempting to comfort them.[31] Thus, it appears that although younger children frequently may be interested in others and willing to comfort them, adolescents are more able (or at least more likely) to respond in optimal ways.

Preadolescents and adolescents are also likely to sympathize with and comfort a wider range of people than are younger children. Hoffman has argued that the ability to sympathize with the distresses of others who are abstract—that is, who are not in the immediate situation—and with the chronic distress of others develops in late childhood or early adolescence. This capability is believed to be based upon the individual's newfound ability to view others as having personal identities and life experiences beyond the immediate situation.[32] If Hoffman is correct, we would expect adolescents to be more sympathetic than children, and therefore more prosocial toward members of disadvantaged groups and other individuals whose distress is chronic or not immediately observable.

SHARING AND HELPING

Sharing with people who are not friends or family also increases during the school years. For example, older children are more likely than younger ones to share objects or money with unknown others.[33] Moreover, older children may be slightly more likely to help than younger children[34] and to assist in emergency situations in which someone else is hurt. For example, in one study, one or two children in a room heard another child in a nearby room playing with a game involving a wheel and spokes and catching his or her fingers in the spokes. Then the child in the other room gasped, and emitted cries of distress such as the following, one every 15 seconds. "Oh my finger!" "Oh, rats, it really hurts (sob)"; "I can't get it out, I wish someone would help me."[35] Between the distress cries, labored breathing and a struggle with the machine also could be heard.

In emergency situations involving such an injury or someone else falling, helping behavior seems to increase somewhat with age. However, there is some evidence that helping increases in the mid-elementary-school years, declines later in elementary school or early high school, and then increases again in high school. Interview data from children suggest that young children often are inhibited from helping because they feel unable to assist. In contrast, young adolescents and older preadolescents are inhibited by fear of social disapproval for helping (such as the possibility that their help is not wanted) or fear of embarrassing the potential recipient, as well as by fear of being incompetent as a helper.[36]

Why do older children help more in some situations? Older children have certain skills and knowledge that younger children do not possess. For example, older children will help more than young children on tasks that require experience, such as tying a complex knot, but probably will not help more than younger children when the younger children have been shown how to perform the desired helping behavior. Thus, older children may be more likely to help in some situations simply because they are better able to assist.[37] It is also likely that adolescents help more than younger children when higher levels of role taking (taking the perspective of the other person) are required to discern another's need. However, as was noted previously, older children may not help in some situations because they believe that help would not be effective or appropriate.[38]

Older and younger children also may differ greatly in their reasons for helping. For example, in a study of adolescents' helping, seventh-graders were more likely to assist when a reward or social recognition was offered than when neither was offered, whereas eleventh-graders helped most when they would gain social recognition as a result. Moreover, among those who agreed to assist, eleventh-graders were more likely than seventh- or ninth-graders to report helping for altruistic reasons.[39] This pattern of results suggests that even though younger adolescents sometimes help as much as or more than older ones, they are more likely to assist for nonaltruistic motives such as obtaining a concrete reward.

Infants' and toddlers' understanding of other people's needs and emotional reactions increases dramatically. As a consequence of their newfound understanding and the development of other competencies (for example, the ability to move around and to know where another child's mother is), children exhibit increasing amounts of prosocial behaviors in the second and third years. After that, quantitative gains in prosocial behavior are relatively modest. There is a clear increase in donating behavior during the school years; helping behavior increases somewhat in some settings. School-age children also appear to be somewhat more responsive and sensitive to others' emotional needs than are younger children. In addition, it appears that the *quality* of children's motives for their prosocial behaviors changes considerably with age. We now turn to this issue.

3/ Motives for Prosocial Actions

Prosocial actions are performed for a variety of reasons, ranging from selfish to altruistic ones. Altruistic behaviors differ from nonaltruistic prosocial behaviors in that the former are motivated by moral values or concern for others.

Unfortunately, mere viewing of people's behaviors reveals little or nothing about the underlying motives. For example, a child who assists a peer may do so out of concern for the peer, to get something in return, or to impress an adult.

One way to try to assess children's motivations for helping is to vary situations in ways that are likely to affect certain motivations and then see if and when children assist.[1] For example, researchers can offer rewards or not offer rewards for helping, and see when children actually help.

Even so, different children still may perform the same prosocial behavior in a given setting for different reasons. As an example, consider a situation in which there are no obvious rewards for helping and no adults are present. In this context, one child may donate money, toys, or other valued objects to needy children because of concern for those children. However, other children may donate because they believe that their parents will be proud of them when the children tell them about the donation.

Because observing behavior is at best an indirect way of assessing people's motives, a number of researchers have used interviews to try to understand children's motives for helping, sharing, and other prosocial behaviors. One such procedure is to tap children's conscious motives by asking them why they performed (or did not perform) a given behavior. However, children may not always know why they assisted another or may be unable to verbalize their reasons. Moreover, older children may sometimes give moral-sounding reasons for their behavior that are not genuine, because they want to appear in a positive light to themselves and to the experimenters. Nonetheless, by asking people to explain their own behaviors, it is possible to gain some insight into their motives.

Another way to assess people's reasons for engaging in prosocial behaviors is to assess their moral reasoning by asking them to resolve hypothetical moral dilemmas and justify their decisions. For example, a child may be asked if he or she would help an injured child if doing so required missing a birthday party, and why the child would choose a particular course of action.[2] By assessing an individual's reasoning about a number of such dilemmas, researchers can get a picture of the factors that affect whether or not a given child assists others. Of course, because this method involves self-reporting, it, like self-reports of motives, may be distorted by people's desire to appear in a desirable light and is dependent on the degree to which people are aware of their own motives and are able to verbalize them.[3]

Nonetheless, despite the methodological problems with procedures involving self-reporting of motives and reasoning, such procedures have been very useful in getting a glimpse into children's reasons for enacting prosocial behaviors, and how these reasons change with age. Indeed, the results of studies of children's motives and moral reasoning indicate that the quality of children's prosocial behaviors changes markedly with age.

CHILDREN'S SELF-REPORTED MOTIVES

What kinds of justifications do children provide for their prosocial actions? Consistent with their level of cognitive development, 4- to-5-year-olds' justifications tend to be quite simple, and children's justifications become more complex and varied with age.

PRESCHOOLERS

In studies of preschoolers, we have asked children about their motivations for their own naturally occurring prosocial behaviors in the classroom. When an adult experimenter saw children share or help another person, the adult approached them and asked why they did so (for example, "Johnny, can you tell me why you gave some clay to Susan?"). Preschoolers most often justified their behavior with a simple reference to either the other person's needs (needs-oriented justifications) or pragmatic reasons. Consider the following examples:

> David went over and wiped the table after Aaron had asked him to help with that task. When asked why he did so, he said, "I wiped the table because it was wet" (pragmatic reasoning).

> Sandy gave some of the beads she was stringing to Katie. When asked why, she said, "She wanted some" (needs-oriented justification).

> Robert gave Dan some of his crackers during snack time. His reason, when asked, was "He's hungry" (needs-oriented justification).

Needs-oriented justifications frequently appear to reflect an other-orientation—a focus on the other person's needs.[4] Thus, even young children often seem to be motivated by an understanding of—and perhaps an emotional response to—another's situation and needs. At other times children appear to focus primarily on the task at hand or other practical aspects of the situation.

In addition, 4- and 5-year-olds occasionally justify their prosocial actions with references to their liking of, or relationship with, the recipient of aid (affectional relationship justification), their desire for others' approval (approval-oriented justifications), and self-gain (hedonistic or direct reciprocity justifications).

> Barbie asked Troy to help her carry some toys across the room. He did so, and his reason for helping, when asked, was "She's my friend" (affectional relationship justification).

> Sam helped Jerry to tie the strings on an apron. His reason was "I like him" (affectional relationship justification).

> Tori gave Jack some blocks when Jack asked for some. When asked why she did so, Tori, said, "He'll like me" (approval-oriented justification).

> Steven saved Eric's seat for him at Eric's request. His reason: "He'll save it for me next time" (direct reciprocity).

> Ann asked Sharon to give her some crayons. Sharon did so, and said that she shared because "If I share, the teacher will let me make popcorn later" (hedonistic justification).

Interestingly, American middle-class children rarely justified their prosocial behaviors with overtly selfish reasons. They verbalized self-oriented reasons (hedonistic and direct reciprocity justifications) approximately 4 to 12 percent of the time.[5] The low frequency of self-oriented self-reported motives apparently was not a result of reluctance to verbalize socially unacceptable hedonistic motives; as we shall see shortly, preschoolers often express hedonistic reasons for choosing not to assist.

Preschool children express somewhat different motives for complying with peers' and teachers' requests for sharing or helping. They are likely to justify complying with peers' requests with references to others' needs or to the relationship between oneself and the other (affectional relationship justifications). In contrast, they are much more likely to refer to authorities' dictates and punishment when explaining why they complied with teachers' requests (for example, "Because the teacher told me I had to"). Thus, children's descriptions of their peer-directed compliant prosocial acts seem to be more other-oriented and based on relationships (liking, friendship) than their prosocial actions toward teachers.[6] This pattern of findings is consistent with some theorists' suggestions that adult-child relationships are characterized by compliance and obedience, whereas peer relationships are characterized by interactions involving more egalitarian and prosocial concepts.[7] Peer interactions seem to be an ideal context for children to learn about others' needs and wants and social interchange. We return to this issue in Chapter 8.

ELEMENTARY SCHOOL CHILDREN

Although young children often express other-oriented justifications for helping, a sizable body of research indicates that children's reasons for assisting become somewhat more altruistic with age. In a number of studies, school-age children were given a series of opportunities to help or share with another child. These opportunities varied in ways related to different motives for assisting; for example, rewards were offered for assisting in one situation but not in another. In addition, if and when children assisted, they were questioned about their motives for doing so.[8]

For example, in one study, kindergarteners and second- and fourth-graders played a game with a peer, won candy as a prize, and then were provided with a number of opportunities to share the candy with the peer who had lost (the sequence of opportunities ended when the child shared).[9] The conditions in which the children could share (in order of occurrence) were as follows: (1) altruistic condition (the child was left alone for 3 minutes with the loser); (2) normative condition (the child could share after the experimenter explicitly and at length referred to the norm of sharing; for example, the adult experimenter talked about how good children share and told the child that it is nice to share); (3) internal initiative and concrete reward (the experimenter told the child that he or she would get a reward for sharing); (4) compliance (the experimenter told the winner to share with the loser and moved aside for a couple of minutes); and (5) compliance and concrete-defined reinforcement (the experimenter told the winner to share and promised a big prize for sharing). After children shared in any of the above conditions, they were interviewed about their reasons for doing so.

In such studies older children generally are more likely than younger children to exhibit "higher-quality" prosocial behavior; that is, they are more likely to assist without being told to do so or before being offered concrete rewards.[10] Their self-reported motives for assisting also tend to become more sophisticated and less self-focused with age.[11] Younger children, especially kindergarteners, are more likely than older children to say that they assisted to obtain a prize or rewards. Younger children report altruistic, internal, or clearly empathic motives relatively infrequently, but references to these motives increase with age.[12] For example, older children are more likely than younger children to say "I like to share to give others satisfaction" or "Candy should be shared to make the other children happy." In brief, although even young children frequently may be motivated to help others as a result of sympathy or recognition of others' needs, especially in naturally occurring peer interactions, older children may do so more often. Moreover, older children appear to engage in more actions based on other-oriented motives and self-aware perspective taking.

Also, older children's *failures* to help may often involve different motives from those of younger children. As was discussed in Chapter 2, in a study of helping in an emergency (when another person appeared to be injured), more adolescents than younger children reported being hesitant to help for fear that the recipient would disapprove, be embarrassed, or regard the help as condescending.[13] Younger children reported not helping because they perceived themselves as incompetent. Similarly, when asked about times when they failed to help others in real-life situations, adolescents frequently cited reluctance to interfere in another's personal situation or to violate internalized values, laws, or rules (for example, "I wouldn't help someone with a personal problem that was none of my business" or "I wouldn't help someone do something that I think is wrong"). In contrast, elementary school children were more likely to cite their own incompetence as a justification for not helping (for example, "I wouldn't help him fix a flat tire because I don't know what to do").[14]

Thus, older children's reasons for not helping appear to be somewhat more likely than younger children's to be based on consideration of another's situation or moral values.

THE DEVELOPMENT OF PROSOCIAL MORAL REASONING

Research on prosocial moral reasoning shows that children's moral reasoning about situations involving opportunities for prosocial behavior also changes with age. These changes are illustrated in children's discussions of why they would or would not assist others.

In investigations of moral reasoning, people are presented with moral dilemmas, and asked what should be done and why. For example, Lawrence Kohlberg and his colleagues asked children and adults to reason about situations in which justice and wrongdoing are focal issues (such as a situation in which a man must choose between stealing a drug to save his wife's life and allowing her to die).[15] A typical prosocial moral reasoning dilemma used with young children is as follows (with the gender of the story characters matched to that of the child hearing the story):

> One day while John was playing in his yard, he saw a bully push and tease another child whom he did not know. There weren't any adults around. As John watched, the one boy kept pushing the other boy down every time he tried to get back up. John was having a good time playing in his yard, and the bully might pick on him too if he tried to help.

Preschool children use primarily hedonistic reasoning when discussing dilemmas of this sort, although they also use quite a lot of needs-oriented reasoning. During

the elementary school years, children's reasoning typically becomes somewhat more based on an explicit other-orientation, and more tied to what is perceived as good behavior by other people and by society. In adolescence, reasoning begins to be based on internalized values, role taking, and sympathy. Consider the following responses to the situation presented above by a boy who was interviewed at several ages from preschool to adolescence (only the most important parts of the interview are quoted):

Age 5 years

Interviewer:	What should he do?
Child:	He should stay in his yard.
Interviewer:	Why is that?
Child:	He'll get pushed over. (A very similar answer also was provided at age 6.)

Age 8 years

Interviewer:	What do you think John should do?
Child:	Help him.
Interviewer:	How come?
Child:	So the bully won't hurt him. So he won't get pushed down and stuff.

Age 10 years

Interviewer:	What do you think John should do?
Child:	Well, if there aren't any grownups around he should just go and try to stop the bully.
Interviewer:	Why do you think he would want to go and try to stop the bully?

Child: Because he might not like the bully, and
                  not want the other kid to get hurt.

Interviewer: Why do you think he might not like the
                  bully?

Child: Because he might push his friends
                  around . . . [He'd help] because it would
                  be two on one and if the bully pushes
                  one down the other boy can help him
                  and get the bully.

Age 16 years

Interviewer: What do you think John should do?

Child: Just go help the other child because I
                  don't think he really wants to see him
                  get hurt or anything and he can always
                  just go back and play by himself or with
                  another child . . . It's not right just for
                  anybody to go pick on anybody else.

Interviewer: Tell me more what you mean by that, by
                  it's not right.

Child: People shouldn't just pick on each other;
                  they should have fun with each other,
                  not hurt each other physically or
                  mentally or anything . . . This is just the
                  way that humans should act toward each
                  other—that they are all equal. None of
                  us are bigger than each other so they
                  should treat each other the same. . .
                  Cause you shouldn't really want that
                  child to get hurt because you might get
                  hurt if the situation was switched. Then
                  I think you would want the other child
                  to help you.

This child's reasoning progressed from being self-
focused to focusing on the other child's needs, and then
to focusing on the equality of people, the desirability of

positive interpersonal interactions, and perspective taking.

Here are some responses from the same child to a dilemma in which he had to choose between going to a party and assisting another child who had injured his leg:

Age 5 years

Interviewer: What do you think he [the story protagonist] should do?

Child: Go to the party.

Interviewer: Why is that?

Child: Because he doesn't want to be late.

Interviewer: Why doesn't he want to be late?

Child: Cause then it'd be over.

Age 6 years

Interviewer: What do you think Eric should do?

Child: Go to the party.

Interviewer: And why do you think Eric should do that?

Child: Cause he better so he doesn't miss all the ice cream and cake.

Age 10 years

Interviewer: What do you think Eric should do?"

Child: Go get the boy's parents.

Interviewer: Why do you think he would want to get his parents for him?

Child: Because he doesn't want him to have a broken leg and he wants him to get him to a doctor or hospital real fast because he doesn't want him to get a broken leg or anything worse.

Age 16 years

Interviewer: What do you think Eric should do?

Child: He should go get the parents of the child. It could be a lot serious, even more serious, than what the child thinks. It could be a sprain but it could be a major break and the child can't go get the parents because he might be injured worse. If he was in that situation, he would want somebody to help him too.

This child's responses are fairly typical of other children, with the exception that many children express more needs-oriented and less hedonistic reasoning at age 6. However, even among adolescents, the decision not to assist another person is frequently justified by selfish concerns. In addition, among children in late elementary school, stereotypic reasoning—comments like "It'd be the nice thing to do" or "He'd be mean if he didn't help"—are more common than is evident in this boy's reasoning.[16]

In general, then, children's moral reasoning seems to go through a sequence of changes from the late preschool years into adolescence. Preschoolers use much hedonistic reasoning and needs-oriented reasoning. In elementary school, children's judgments begin to reflect concern with others' approval and stereotypic conceptions of "good" and "bad" behavior. In contrast, high school students frequently verbalize reasoning reflecting self-reflective empathy (role taking, sympathy, concern with the consequences of one's behavior for others); moreover, they use modest amounts of reasoning reflecting abstract principles and internalized affective reactions (for example, guilt or positive affect relating to living up to one's principles and feeling good about doing so; see Table 1).

Table 1. Levels of prosocial reasoning

Level 1. Hedonistic, self-focused orientation: The individual is concerned with self-oriented consequences rather than moral considerations. Reasons for assisting or not assisting another include consideration of direct gain to the self, future reciprocity, and concern for others because one needs and/or likes the other (as a result of the affectional tie.) (Predominant mode primarily for preschoolers and younger elementary-school children.)

Level 2. Needs-oriented orientation: The individual expresses concern for the physical, material, and psychological needs of others even though these needs conflict with one's own. This concern is expressed in the simplest terms, without clear evidence of self-reflective role taking, verbal expressions of sympathy, or reference to internalized affect such as guilt. (Predominant mode for many preschoolers and many elementary-school children.)

Level 3. Approval and interpersonal orientation and/or stereotyped orientation: Stereotyped images of good and bad persons and behaviors and/or considerations of others' approval and acceptance are used in justifying prosocial or nonhelping behaviors. (Predominant mode for some elementary- and high-school students.)

Level 4a. Self-reflecting empathic orientation: The individual's judgments include evidence of self-reflective sympathetic responding or role taking, concern with the other's humanness, or guilt or positive feelings related to the consequences of one's actions. (Predominant mode for a few older elementary-school children and many high-school students.)

Level 4b. Transitional level: The individual's justifications for helping or not helping involve internalized values, norms, duties, or responsibilities, concern for the condition of the larger society, or the necessity of protecting the rights and dignity of other persons; these ideas, however, are not clearly and strongly stated. (Predominant mode for a minority of people high-school age or older.)

Level 5. Strongly internalized stage: Justifications for helping or not helping are based on internalized values, norms, or responsibilities, the desire to maintain individual and societal contractual obligations or to improve the condition of society, a belief in the dignity, rights, and equality of all individuals. Positive or negative feelings related to the maintenance of self-respect for living up to one's own values and accepted norms also characterize this stage. (Predominant mode for only a small minority of high-school students and no elementary-school children.)

Source: Nancy Eisenberg, *Altruistic Emotion, Cognition, and Behavior* (Hillsdale, N.J.: Lawrence Erlbaum Associates, 1986).

Similar changes in moral reasoning have been found among elementary school children in Germany and Japan.[17] However, cultural and subcultural factors do seem to affect prosocial reasoning to some degree. For example, children in ideological subcultures such as the kibbutz society in Israel express more sophisticated reasoning than do Americans, whereas older children and adults in nonwestern, rural cultures typically use simple other-oriented modes of reasoning more than people in Western cultures do (see Chapter 6).[18]

Overall, then, children's reasons and justifications for prosocial behaviors become more altruistic with age. This does not mean that older children are always more helpful than younger children, or that they always act in accordance with the values and ideas they profess. However, older children do seem more capable than younger children of understanding others' perspectives and abstract values pertaining to altruism, as well as the ways in which their behaviors may be viewed by others. The relevance of such understanding for prosocial behavior is considered—along with a number of other issues—in the next chapter.

4/ Characteristics of Prosocial Children

Some children obviously are more prosocial than others. Some children are likely to get tears in their eyes and approach others whom they see in physical pain; some are not. Some children try to comfort others who are upset and have personal problems; others do so less frequently. Certain children are much more likely than others to share their toys and to help other people with tasks when there are no obvious rewards for doing so. Do prosocial children and less prosocial children differ in any personal characteristics other than in prosocial tendencies?

Of course, no child shares, helps, and comforts all the time, and no child is always selfish and self-focused in his or her actions. Differences between prosocial and less prosocial children are not all-or-none. Prosocial children may differ from less prosocial children *in general* on some characteristic, but this does not mean that every prosocial child differs from every nonprosocial child on the particular characteristic in question. When we talk about differences between prosocial and nonprosocial children in characteristics such as sociability and social adjustment, we are talking about differences in the *average* prosocial child in comparison to the *average* nonprosocial child. But not every prosocial child is like most other prosocial child; nor is every self-focused child like the average self-focused child.

As was mentioned in Chapter 2, older children tend to be more prosocial—at least in some ways—than younger ones; therefore, prosocial children may tend to be older than less prosocial children. In what other ways do prosocial and nonprosocial children differ?

Parents, teachers, students, and professionals interested in children tend to entertain stereotypes about helpful children and selfish, unhelpful ones. Many people tend to view girls as being more prosocial than boys, and generous, helpful children are often seen as being sociable and adjusted.[1] In addition, people generally think of prosocial children as being sympathetic, as being relatively skilled at taking the perspectives of others, and as having a repertoire of socially competent problem-solving skills that can be used in social conflict situations. We might also wonder if prosocial children are more intelligent than other children, if they tend to come from large or small families, and if they are first- or later-born children.

Why is it important to pinpoint differences in the personal characteristics of highly prosocial and less prosocial children? If we have some information about differences among children who differ in level of prosocial responding, we can start to understand some of the factors that may underlie prosocial responding. For example, if prosocial children are more sympathetic than other children and are better at taking the perspectives of others, it would seem reasonable to conclude that sympathy and perspective-taking skills might play some role in prosocial responding.

Of course, the mere fact that prosocial children are more sympathetic than less prosocial children does not in itself prove that sympathy is a cause of prosocial behavior. Nonetheless, if there are theoretical reasons to believe that a personal characteristic (such as sympathy) that is correlated with prosocial responding does have some effect on prosocial responding, it is useful to examine the relation further, for at least two reasons. First, if there is reason to believe that certain personal characteristics enhance the likelihood of children's behaving in a prosocial manner, it may be possible to use this information when trying to understand why some cultural factors and childrearing techniques seem to increase children's prosocial tendencies. For example, if we know that sympathetic children help and share more than other children, we can consider ways in which particular childrearing techniques associated with prosocial outcomes in children may foster sympathetic responding. Second, if it is fairly clear that certain types of children are more caring and generous than others, we can develop intervention programs in the home, school, and other settings that capitalize on this information. Such information can be used to design intervention procedures that are likely to enhance the particular characteristic (such as sympathy), with the hope that the intervention will also have an effect on children's prosocial behavior.

Several aspects of children's personality and background have been examined in relation to prosocial behavior. The first consists of demographic variables such as sex of the child, the child's ordinal position in the family (whether the child is first- or later-born), and the socioeconomic status of the child's family. A second aspect concerns the child's social style (for example, sociability) and ability to cope in social contexts. A third pertains to the child's emotional responsiveness to others—that is, the child's sympathetic and empathic responsiveness. A fourth type of characteristic examined is personal capabilities indicative of cognitive development, such as intelligence quotient (IQ) and the ability to take another's perspective.

One other issue important to consider is whether children exhibit any consistency in their prosocial behavior. Although it seems as if some children are more altruistic than others, it is possible that children are so inconsistent in their behavior in different settings that there are no reliable individual differences. It would be a waste of time to discuss differences between prosocial and non-prosocial children if some children did not tend to be more prosocial than others across a variety of settings. Thus the question must be addressed: Are some children more likely than others to exhibit sharing, caring, and helping across a number of contexts?

CONSISTENCY

The answer seems to be yes. Although any given child may share in one situation and not another, or help in one situation and not share in another, in general there is some individual consistency in children's prosocial responding. However, children's consistency in regard to prosocial behavior seems to increase with age. In the first few years of life, consistency in infants' and toddlers' prosocial responding across settings and across time is low.[2] For example, the amount that 24-month-olds share with or comfort siblings or parents varies considerably across settings, with some children being more prosocial in one context and others being more prosocial in another.

In contrast, individual preschoolers and school-age children show moderate consistency in prosocial behaviors.[3] For example, in a longitudinal study, Diana Baumrind collected extensive observations on children in nursery school and then again in elementary school (5–6 years later).[4] In preschool, children's nurturance, sympathy, consideration, and understanding of the perspectives of peers were all intercorrelated in ways that suggested individual differences in an underlying predisposition toward social responsibility and prosocial behavior. Similar associations among prosocial and socially responsible behaviors were found when the children were in elementary school. In addition, children who were socially responsible and prosocial in nursery school tended to be high in these characteristics in elementary school.[5] Thus, Baumrind's data are consistent with the view that there are enduring individual differences in children's prosocial functioning.

Some studies of older elementary school children and adolescents have also shown consistency in prosocial responding.[6] For example, in studies of adolescents' naturally occurring prosocial behaviors on biking and canoeing trips, various measures of prosocial behavior such as helping a peer to put up a tent or sharing possessions were interrelated. Moreover, individual differences in level of prosocial behavior were consistent over several weeks.[7]

Children's styles of dealing with potential helping situations also seem to be somewhat stable. Marian Radke-Yarrow and Carolyn Zahn-Waxler described the behavior of the 1½- to 2½-year-olds in their study as follows:

> Patterned individuality in the quality of responding to the distress of others becomes evident very early. Thus certain children, as their reactions are plotted over time, stand out as affectively prosocial. Their prosocial responding has a large component of emotional arousal. They are seldom described in ways that suggest careful cognitive processing, reflection, or problem solving. In contrast, other children who progress

equally in complex and effective prosocial intervention manifest prosocial behavior that is without apparent strong emotional underpinnings. They appear to be approaching the distress "cognitively"—by inspecting, exploring, asking questions. Other children have an aggressive component in their prosocial interactions (hitting the person who made the baby cry; hitting at one of the parents in the midst of the parents' quarrel; tearing up the newspaper that made his mother cry). Others shut out signals of distress and turn or run away.[8]

Not only did the children tend to exhibit individual differences in style of response at an early age, but these individual differences were relatively stable over time. When a number of the children were studied again 5 years later at approximately age 7, two-thirds exhibited the same style of dealing with others' distresses. This finding suggests that there are consistencies in qualitative aspects of people's prosocial behaviors, as well as in the amount that they share, help, or comfort.

Of course, we should not expect even a very altruistic person to assist in all situations or always to help in the same way. A man who is good at comforting may have little money to share or may value his money more than his time. Practical considerations such as people's resources and competencies certainly affect whether or not they help, share, or comfort in a given situation. In addition, not all prosocial actions are performed for the same reasons; some are performed for altruistic reasons, whereas others may be performed merely to obtain a reward or social approval. Certain prosocial behaviors are performed because a child feels sorry for another; other prosocial behaviors are enacted because the child is unable to refuse a request to assist. Prosocial actions that are performed for different reasons are not likely to be highly correlated across settings.

In summary, it appears that there are stable individual differences in prosocial behavior, including altruistic behavior. Some people are more prosocial than others in a variety of contexts (though not in all). Thus, it is reasonable to try to delineate some of the differences in the demographic characteristics, personality, and emotional and cognitive functioning of altruistic and less altruistic children.

GENDER DIFFERENCES

Despite the stereotype that girls share, help, and comfort other people more than boys do, most studies of gender differences in children's prosocial behaviors have found no difference between boys and girls. However, when differences have been found, they appear to be slightly more likely to favor females.[9]

Even when differences favoring girls have been found, they may not reflect true differences in prosocial responding. Girls tend to be viewed as more prosocial by others, and therefore may be rated as more helpful by teachers and peers even if they really are not.[10] Indeed, males may be more helpful than females when helping involves instrumental rescuing or helping behaviors (for example, helping to change a flat tire) or potential danger (for example, picking up a hitchhiker). In contrast, girls and women may be more likely to help when psychological assistance (for example, comforting) is needed, and when the recipient of help is an acquaintance, friend, or child.[11]

In summary, although girls may perform some types of prosocial behaviors more than boys do, there are no clear sex differences in prosocial behavior. If there is any difference favoring girls, it may stem from the fact that in many cultures, nurturance and helpfulness are considered to be more appropriate for females. In fact there is some evidence that girls may be reinforced for prosocial behavior more than boys are.[12] However, with age, boys may receive more approval than girls do for performing helping behaviors that involve risk, physical tasks, or aiding females (that is, are chivalrous).

DEMOGRAPHIC CHARACTERISTICS

SOCIAL CLASS

Social class does not appear to be consistently related to children's prosocial behavior.[13] However, boys from entrepreneurial, middle-class families may be somewhat less prosocial than other middle-class boys and more likely than other children to consider reciprocity—helping someone who has already helped or may help them in the future—as a principal reason for offering assistance.[14] This finding, if correct, suggests that children learn about when to help from observing the work world and attitudes of their parents.

FAMILY SIZE AND ORDINAL POSITION

A common perception is that children in large families are especially likely to be helpful because of the need for them to assist with raising siblings and other family-related tasks. In fact, children from small families assist more in some contexts, and those from large families help more in others.[15] Although children in large families may be particularly likely to assist their siblings, currently there is little research that can be used to support or refute this possibility.

Similarly, research findings in the United States and similar countries regarding the prosocial behavior of first- and later-born children are not consistent across studies.[16] However, observations of real-life behavior in six cultures showed that only children and the youngest child in a family tended to be more likely than other children to seek help and attention, and less likely to offer help and support.[17] In addition, it is clear that older siblings assist their younger siblings much more often than the reverse, and that more prosocial behavior occurs between siblings when they are widely spaced in age.[18] It is likely that these patterns reflect parents' expectations that older children will assist with their younger siblings as well as the fact that older children are better able than younger siblings to assist when the later-born sibling is young, especially if there is a large difference in the siblings' ages.

SOCIABILITY AND ADJUSTMENT

Children with certain personalities appear to be more prosocial than other children. Among the traits most often linked to helpfulness, caring, and generosity are sociability and adjustment.

Children who freely express their feelings and who are relatively social seem to be particularly likely to approach and to assist peers. For example, among toddlers, preschoolers, and school-age children, the expression of emotion—especially positive emotion—is associated with prosocial actions in the classroom or other settings.[19] Moreover, gregarious children engage in more prosocial behavior than do shyer children, especially in behavior outside the home, and especially in behavior that is offered spontaneously.[20] Indeed, sociable children often seem to share and help as a mechanism for initiating social interaction with another peer:

> Sara was watching Doris and Nora playing with the tea set. When Doris started looking for plates to use for serving cookies in her pretend play, Sara found some

plates and brought them to Doris and Nora. When she gave them the plates, she spoke to them and laughed, and then joined in their play.

Introverted children frequently may not help simply because they want to avoid social interaction or attention. In one study, sixth graders, alone or in pairs, were in a room and heard an "emergency" in a nearby room (they actually heard a tape recording of another child who apparently was injured). If the children were alone when they heard the emergency, introverted and extroverted children helped equally. However, if two children were in the room, the extroverted children engaged in more active helping (for example, trying to go to assist), whereas the introverted children tended to prefer modes of helping that did not require social interaction with a peer (for example, giving information about the emergency to an adult or seeking adult assistance).[21]

Among preschoolers, assertiveness, often in the form of mild aggression, seems to be associated with relatively high levels of prosocial behavior.[22] Assertive preschoolers—those likely to defend objects in their possession and to take toys from peers—are particularly likely to help and share spontaneously. Moreover, assertiveness in the elementary school years is associated with relatively high levels of prosocial responding. A certain level of dominance and assertiveness may be necessary for many children to approach other people spontaneously and offer help.[23] However, highly aggressive preschool and school-age children tend not to be prosocial.[24] High levels of aggression and overt aggression more likely reflect hostile motives and should not be confused with the mild, low-level aggression that is often apparent in young children's play.

Whereas assertive children tend to offer help and possessions to others spontaneously, children low in assertiveness often are asked for help or objects, and frequently comply when asked. Children who are unlikely to assert themselves may be seen as easy targets by their peers.[25] Such children frequently may comply with peers' requests simply because it is difficult for them to deal with social conflict.

Consistent with the findings that sociable, assertive children are particularly likely to assist others spontaneously, preschoolers and elementary school children who are relatively prosocial tend to be well adjusted and good at coping with stress.[26] In addition, children's donating, helping, and consideration for others have been associated with teachers' ratings of children's competence with peers, popularity, and having a close friend. Those preadolescents viewed as altruistic by their peers report high levels of self-esteem and satisfaction with their relationships with peers, whereas unpopular adolescents engage in relatively low levels of prosocial behavior.[27]

Overall, then, the results from a variety of studies suggest that children with strong prosocial predispositions tend to be emotionally expressive, socially skilled, assertive, and well adjusted. However, there is only a limited amount of research available on this topic—not all of which is consistent—so conclusions must be tentative. For example, some children with emotional problems may be quite prosocial, perhaps because they themselves overract to others' distresses or try to use prosocial actions to "buy friendship."[28] It is probable, however, that well-adjusted children are more likely than less adjusted children to perform prosocial behaviors for other-oriented, altruistic reasons.

VICARIOUS EMOTIONAL RESPONSIVENESS

For centuries, some philosophers have noted the role of empathy and sympathy in altruism. For example, David Hume argued that sympathy and empathy (called benevolence, sympathy, or humanity) play a major role in morality:

> Here is a principle, which accounts, in great part, for the origin of morality: And what need we seek for abstruse and remote systems, when there occurs one so obvious and natural? . . . Have we any difficulty to comprehend the force of humanity and benevolence? Or to conceive, that the very aspect of happiness, joy, and prosperity, gives pleasure; that of pain, suffering, sorrow, communicates uneasiness? . . . The signs of sorrow and mourning, though arbitrary, affect us with melancholy; but the natural symptoms, tears and cries and groans, never fail to infuse compassion and uneasiness. And if the effects of misery touch us in so lively a manner, can we be supposed altogether insensible or indifferent towards its causes; when a malicious or treacherous character and behaviour are presented to us?[29]

In recent years, numerous psychologists also have argued that altruism often is motivated by empathy or sympathy. In much of this research, *empathy* is defined as an emotional reaction to another's emotional state or condition that is consistent with the others' state or condition (for example, feeling sad when viewing a sad person), whereas *sympathy* is defined as feelings of concern or sorrow for another in reaction to the other's emotional state or condition.[30] In general, people who experience another's distress or sadness and feel concern for the distressed or needy person are expected to be motivated to alleviate the cause of the other person's sadness or distress.

However, not all emotional reactions to others' distress are likely to lead to prosocial behavior. Sometimes people observing others in distress or in need experience an aversive, self-focused reaction such as anxiety or discomfort, and are motivated primarily to alleviate their own, rather than the other person's, aversive emotional state. This sort of emotional response, called *personal distress*, seems to be associated with egoistic rather than other-oriented motives. People experiencing personal distress are expected to assist only when assisting is the easiest way to make themselves feel less distressed, that is, when it is difficult to escape contact with the needy or distressed other who is causing them to feel distressed and when assisting is not highly costly. In contrast, people experiencing personal distress are expected to leave rather than help if it is easy to escape from the distressed person and the aversive cues emitted by that person.[31]

Sympathy and empathy seem to be linked to prosocial behavior, even among very young children. Consider the behavior of the following 20-month-old boy:

> When a visiting friend who was about to leave burst into tears, complaining that her parents were not home (they were away for 2 weeks), his immediate reaction was to look sad, but then he offered her his beloved teddy bear to take home. His parents reminded him that he would miss the teddy if he gave it away, but he insisted.[32]

This boy exhibited sadness and sympathy when he viewed his friend crying, and then offered her a valued toy in an attempt to comfort her.

The association of sympathy with prosocial behavior is especially clear in studies of adults. For example, in a study of Europeans who helped rescue Jews during World War II, rescuers and people from the same locale who had not engaged in rescuing activities were interviewed. When asked about their motives for rescuing Jews, more than half the rescuers reported that they helped primarily because they sympathized and empathized with the victims they rescued.[33]

In many experimental laboratory studies of sympathy and personal distress, some adults are placed in circumstances in which they are likely to experience empathy and sympathy. In such studies, people in sympathy-eliciting circumstances generally are more likely to help others than are those adults who are in situations that are less likely to induce empathy or sympathy. For example, adults who are instructed to try to take the perspective of another person in a radio or television broadcast are more likely to want to help a needy person in that broadcast than are people who are told to watch the film in an objective manner. Similarly, adults who report on questionnaires that they are relatively likely to respond sympathetically and empathically are especially likely to engage in prosocial actions; for example, they are more likely than people who describe themselves as low in sympathy and empathy to offer to spend time doing chores for a women whose children are in the hospital (so that she can spend time visiting and tutoring her children). However, adults experiencing personal distress assist relatively little if they do not have to continue contact with the other person in distress.[34]

The results of research with children are not as consistent as the findings for adults; nonetheless, they do support the view that there is some relation between children's sympathy and empathy and their attempts to assist other people. However, whether or not empathy is associated with children's prosocial behavior seems to depend on the method used to assess empathy. In most studies, empathy in children has been assessed with what are called picture-story measures. With these measures, children are shown stories and/or pictures containing information about another's emotional state or situation (for example, a child who lost his dog). Then the children are asked to report, either verbally or by pointing to pictures of facial expressions, what they themselves are feeling. Children are scored as empathizing if they report experiencing the emotion that the story protagonist would be expected to feel.[35]

Empathy as assessed with picture-story measures has not been positively related to children's prosocial behavior. There may be several explanations for this result. For one thing, the stories used to evoke emotion may be too short to elicit an emotional response from the children. In addition, with such procedures, it is likely that children try to give the expected or desired response (that is, say they feel empathic) even if they really feel nothing when they hear the stories. Other potential problems include the possibility that children are not able to shift their emotions as quickly as they are shifted from story to story, and the fact that children score higher on empathy with picture-story measures if interviewed by a same-sex experimenter. Thus, it is quite possible that picture-story measures of empathy have not been positively related to prosocial behavior because they are not valid indexes of empathy.[36]

The pattern of findings is different when physiological responses and nonverbal facial reactions to sympathy-evoking events have been used as markers of children's emotional responsiveness to others. Children who exhibit empathy nonverbally often are more helpful and generous than children who do not. For example, 1-year-olds who exhibit facial sadness in response to viewing a sad adult appear to be more prosocial at home (according to parental report).[37] Similar results also have been found with older children. For example, in one study, children viewed one or two films on two different days, one week apart. In each film, a boy and a girl were playing on local playgrounds and then hurt themselves. The actors in the two films were different pairs of children. The children viewing the films were told that the events in the film were real, and their facial and gestural reactions to the films were videotaped and coded for negative emotion. The preschoolers also were given an opportunity to help the injured children in one film by making a game for them to play in the hospital. However, such helping was costly to the children; the preschoolers could *either* help or play with attractive toys. Moreover, on another day, the children were given the opportunity to donate attractive stickers to needy children whom they did not know.

For both boys and girls, those who exhibited negative affect in response to viewing the injured children were more prosocial. Boys who exhibited more empathy were especially likely to assist the hospitalized children; empathic girls donated more than did less empathic girls.[38] In addition, in another similar study, preschoolers whose faces showed more sadness and concern while watching a videotape of injured peers were those who more often spontaneously offered to share when playing with a peer and one attractive toy.[39]

Heart rates have also been used as markers of children's vicarious emotional responding. In a typical study, preschoolers or elementary school children view a purported pilot television show from the local public broadcasting station about a sister and brother who have injured themselves (in a car accident or by falling from a tree house when a tree branch broke) and need assistance, or a documentary film about a real child with spina bifida. Then the children are given an opportunity to assist the needy child (or children) in the film. Typically, the children's heart-rate responses to the evocative part of the films are associated with prosocial responding. In general, heart-rate deceleration, an index of outward orientation and a marker of sympathy, is associated with higher levels of prosocial responding, whereas heart-rate acceleration, a marker of anxiety and personal distress, is associated with low levels. In addition, children whose faces show concern or sadness when they view the needy children's situations, particularly the boys, seem especially prone to assist other people. In contrast, boys whose faces exhibit personal distress are somewhat less likely to assist. Thus, although the pattern of findings is not always apparent for both sexes or all age groups, the research findings suggest that children who experience sympathy rather than personal distress are relatively likely to help.[40]

In summary, children who are sympathetic and empathic seem to be especially likely to engage in prosocial actions. However, not all prosocial behavior is motivated by sympathy or empathy. In some situations in which people can or do help, the recipient of assistance is not needy or distressed, or there are no cues indicating that the other person is in distress. In such contexts, prosocial actions would not be expected to be motivated by sympathy, and sympathetic children may be no more likely to assist than other children. Nonetheless, sympathetic, emotionally responsive youngsters appear to be more likely to assist when it is clear that another person is distressed or needs assistance.

COGNITIVE CHARACTERISTICS

Thus far, we have seen that prosocial children tend to be sociable and socially competent, well adjusted, and emotionally responsive to others. But do prosocial children differ from other children in their intelligence and in cognitively based abilities such as the ability to take others' perspectives or moral reasoning? More intelligent children may be more able to discern other people's needs and to devise methods of assisting others, but that does not mean they will do so. Moreover, in many situations in which a person can assist someone else, a high level of cognitive functioning may not be required to discern the other person's need or distress and to assist. Thus, although the development of cognitive abilities in the first 2 years of life is undoubtedly related to children's ability to respond appropriately to other persons in distress (see Chapter 2), cognitive abilities per se might not be expected to play as great a role in prosocial functioning in childhood.

GENERAL INTELLIGENCE

Do smart children help, comfort, or share more than other children? The answer seems to be a qualified yes. Although a number of studies have not established an association between measures of cognitive ability and prosocial behavior, overall there appeared to be a modest positive association between children's prosocial behavior and their scores on tests of general cognitive ability (for example IQ tests or tests of logical reasoning). Thus, it appears that intelligence probably facilitates prosocial behavior in some subset of contexts, possibly those in which it is difficult to detect the other person's need or to figure out how to help.[41]

PERSPECTIVE TAKING

Many theorists, investigators, and professionals working with children have argued that the ability to take others' perspectives—that is, to understand their thoughts, feelings, and point of view—is a prerequisite to altruism, or at least frequently motivates altruistic behavior. The empirical date suggests that perspective taking does play a role in prosocial behavior, but that it may not be a prerequisite of prosocial behavior (or even of altruism) in all contexts.

As was discussed in Chapter 2, even young children exhibit some ability to understand others' perspectives, although perspective-taking abilities increase with age.[42] Martin Hoffman has argued that the development of perspective-taking abilities enables even young children to engage in appropriate helping behaviors. Consider the following example of a 15-month-old's behavior when his friend Paul started crying during a struggle over a toy:

> Michael appeared disturbed and let go, but Paul still cried. Michael paused, then brought his teddy bear to Paul but to no avail. Michael paused again, and then finally succeeded in stopping Paul's crying by fetching Paul's security blanket from an adjoining room.[43]

In this incident, Michael appeared to be able to figure out how Paul felt about his security blanket, even though the blanket probably provided no security for Michael.

Clearly, simple perspective-taking abilities are important for figuring out how other people feel and what makes them feel differently. Thus, Hoffman is probably correct in asserting that developments in the ability to take others' perspectives underlie some of the changes in prosocial responding seen in the first few years of life (see Chapter 2).

The association of perspective-taking abilities with prosocial behavior is probably more limited after the first years of life; nonetheless, preschool and elementary school children who exhibit perspective-taking skills are somewhat more likely than other children to assist or share.[44] In a number of studies, investigators have assessed children's understanding of other people's feelings and thoughts and examined the relation of children's scores on these tests to their prosocial behavior. For example, in one study, second graders were classified as high or low in perspective-taking ability on the basis of three tests designed to assess children's perspective taking. In these tests, children were asked to make inferences about the intentions of a character in a story, to label and explain the story protagonists' affective states (for example, to indicate if a wife and husband in a story were angry or bored), and tell a cartoon story from the perspective of another person who had less information about the story than did the children themselves. Prosocial behavior was assessed from videotapes of the children teaching two kindergarteners to make caterpillars with construction paper, scissors, glue, and crayons. Children who were high in perspective-taking abilities were more responsive to the kindergarteners' questions and were more likely to offer to assist them than were children low in perspective taking. The high perspective takers also were more likely to respond to indirect requests for help, a finding that suggests that they were more attuned than low perspective takers to the kindergarteners' needs.[45]

Although perspective taking fosters children's prosocial behavior in some situations, it is not a prerequisite of prosocial behavior. Often prosocial behaviors are preformed rather automatically without much thought, for example, when someone helps another person waiting in a line to pick up dropped objects. In addition, sometimes perspective taking is not necessary for assisting because the other's need is obvious, or because the other person is not really in need. Moreover, people often assist others for self-related reasons, such as the desire for reciprocity or social approval; in such situations, children may not attend to other people's feelings or perspectives. Finally, even when children do take the perspective of other people, they may not always help, either because they are not sufficiently motivated or because the cost of helping is too high. In addition, even if a child takes another individual's perspective and is motivated to help, he or she may lack the skills or confidence to do so.[46] Thus, enhancing children's perspective-taking abilities may not always increase their prosocial behavior.

MORAL REASONING

Moral reasoning is, in part, a cognitive skill. As was discussed in Chapter 3, children's thinking about prosocial moral conflicts undergoes dramatic changes as they get older, and these changes probably reflect age-related advances in cognitive abilities. Moreover, researchers studying a variety of types of moral reasoning have found that IQ, tests of academic ability, and logical ability are associated with higher-level moral reasoning.[47] Higher-level moral reasoning simply involves more complex concepts and a better understanding of other people's perspectives than does lower-level reasoning.

Given that higher-level moral reasoning generally is viewed as more adequate morally, it is not surprising that investigators have frequently hypothesized that people who exhibit higher-level moral reasoning also are more likely than other people to exhibit moral behaviors, including altruism. This prediction generally has been supported—especially in regard to prosocial behavior.[48] Although the relation between moral reasoning and prosocial behavior is modest and has not been found in a number of studies, overall it appears that children who reason in terms of their own needs and desires—what they themselves will get out of helping or not helping—are particularly unlikely to share valued possessions or help others. In contrast, children who reason about other individuals' needs and who use higher-level reasoning are particularly likely to share possessions spontaneously, donate valuable objects to others, or help when doing so is costly (for example, when helping requires giving up time playing with attractive toys).[49] In addition, children who give higher-level (that is, more altruistic) justifications for their own moral actions are more likely than other children to assist in contexts in which there are no rewards for helping or no pressure from adults to assist (see Chapter 3).[50]

However, as for perspective taking, higher-level moral reasoning may not be related to, or even relevant to, all prosocial actions. Some actions simply do not involve the consideration of moral issues. For example, we often perform trivial helping behaviors by habit, without much conscious thought; moreover, low-cost prosocial behaviors are unlikely to evoke a moral conflict and therefore would not be expected to elicit morally relevant cognitions. In addition, people may not always act in ways consistent with their moral reasoning. For example, people may not assist as a result of competing motivations such as the desire to complete some other task, shyness, or the lack of a relevant skill (for example, knowledge of first aid).[51]

In conclusion, some children are more prosocial than others, and these children appear to differ from less prosocial children on a variety of personal dimensions. Most notably, children who engage in more prosocial behavior, especially behaviors that appear to be altruistically motivated, tend to exhibit higher-level perspective-taking skills and moral reasoning and are more emotionally responsive to other people in need or distress. This is not surprising; understanding others' perspectives, feeling their distress and concern for their distress, and thinking about the validity of other individuals' needs and relevant moral principles have frequently been cited as the basis of moral behavior, including altruism. In addition, sociable, assertive, socially competent children seem especially likely to engage in some types of prosocial acts, including those that require social initiative. In contrast, nonassertive children may assist primarily when asked, and often they may comply with a request because they have difficulty asserting themselves and coping with social conflicts. Further, intelligent children perform somewhat more prosocial behavior than less intelligent children, probably because they are more able to discern others' needs, use higher-level moral reasoning, and feel more competent to assist. Finally, girls and boys may prefer to engage in somewhat different types of prosocial behavior; for example, females may prefer giving physical or psychological comfort to other people, whereas males may feel more comfortable providing instrumental assistance.

These differences in children's helpfulness, generosity, and comforting behaviors provide clues about the origins of prosocial tendencies. It is to the question of these origins that we now turn.

5/ The Biological Bases of Altruism

We have already seen that even young children are capable of prosocial behavior and genuine concern for others; that there are individual differences in children's prosocial behaviors—some children are more likely than others to share, help, or comfort others; and that these differences tend to be associated with certain personal characteristics. What, then, are the bases of altruism and other forms of prosocial behavior?

Professionals studying children and social behavior have suggested a number of different factors that may cause variation among individuals in helpfulness, generosity, or concern for others. These include biological or genetically based factors, cultural influences, and the socializing effects of family, teachers, peers, and the media. The next few chapters discuss each of these potential influences on children's prosocial behavior. This chapter focuses on biological influences.

The notion that individual differences in prosocial tendencies have a biological basis rests on a more basic assumption—that biological factors affect the prosocial behavior of human beings as a group, regardless of differences among people.

PROSOCIAL BEHAVIOR IN ANIMALS AND HUMANS

If prosocial behavior has a biological basis and is not solely a product of human culture, we would expect to find altruism in animals as well as in humans. And in fact, scientists who study the social behavior of animals and insects have described many examples of helping, sharing, and self-sacrifice among animals.

Edward O. Wilson, a prominent biologist who has argued that altruism has a biological basis, presented a number of examples of animal self-sacrifice in his book *Sociobiology*.[1] Several of these involved social insects. Soldier ants and termites routinely protect the rest of their colony by exposing themselves to great danger when the colony is attacked. Honeybee workers attack those who are a potential threat to their hives by stinging with a barbed stinger that tends to remain in the victim. When the bee pulls away, its viscera are pulled out, and it dies as a result of protecting the group. Certain wasps also perform such self-sacrificial acts and, in Wilson's words, "The fearsome reputation of social bees and wasps is due to their general readiness to throw away their lives upon slight provocation."[2]

Wilson also described altruistic behavior among vertebrates:

> Although vertebrates are seldom suicidal in the manner of the social insects, many place themselves in harm's way to defend relatives. The dominant males of chacma baboon troops *(Papio ursinus)* position themselves in exposed locations in order to scan the environment while the other troop members forage. If predators or rival troops approach, the dominant males warn the others by barking and may move toward the intruders in a threatening way, perhaps accompanied by other

males. As the troop retreats, the dominant males cover the rear . . .

Adult members of one African wild dog pack were observed to attack a cheetah and a hyena, at considerable risk to their own lives, in order to save a pup that could not have been a closer relation than a cousin or a nephew. Unattached Adelie penguins help defend nests and creches of chicks belonging to other birds against the attacks of skuas. The breeding colonies of penguins are so strikingly large and the defending behavior sufficiently broadcast to make it unlikely that the defenders are discriminating closely in favor of relatives.[3]

Prosocial behavior is also observed among many species of birds, particularly when their own or their relatives' offspring are in danger. For example, female birds sometimes try to distract intruders from the nest by feigning injuries. They will land on the ground and grovel frantically or hold one wing as if it were crippled in an attempt to attract the intruder away from the nest toward themselves. Such behavior endangers the female adult's life but protects the young from harm. In addition, birds and other animals such as chimpanzees and wolves sometimes adopt young whose parents have died or are missing.[4]

Numerous animals exhibit sharing behavior as well as helping and protective behaviors. According to Wilson, "Altruistic food sharing among adults is also known among African wild dogs, where it permits some individuals to remain at the dens with the cubs while others hunt . . . The donors carry fresh meat directly to the recipients or else regurgitate it in front of them. Occasionally a mother dog will allow other adults to suckle milk."[5]

Clearly, prosocial behavior is not confined to humans.

This fact has led to an interesting debate among biologists. Because an altruistic animal may lose its life, altruism would not seem to be evolutionarily adaptive. Animals that are maimed or killed assisting others are less likely to mate and pass on their genes. Behaviors that do not increase the likelihood of an individual's reproducing would not be expected to evolve in a species, at least from a Darwinian perspective. How can altruism be explained within an evolutionary framework?

Wilson and other biologists dealt with this apparent paradox by invoking the concept of *kin selection*.[6] They have argued that self-sacrificial behaviors can evolve if the performance of such behaviors increases the probability that the altruist's genes are passed on by its close relatives.

> In the process of natural selection, then, any device that can insert a higher proportion of certain genes into subsequent generations will come to characterize the species. One class of such devices promotes prolonged individual survival. Another promotes superior mating performance and care of the resulting offspring. As more complex social behavior by the organism is added to the genes' techniques of replicating themselves, altruism becomes increasingly prevalent and eventually appears in exaggerated forms. This brings us to the central theoretical problem of sociobiology: how can altruism, which by definition reduces personal fitness, possibly evolve by natural selection? The answer is kinship: if the genes causing the altruism are shared by two organisms because of common descent, and if the altruistic act by one organism increases the joint contribution of these genes to the next generation, the propensity to altruism will spread through the gene pool. This occurs even though the altruist makes less of a solitary contribution to the gene pool as the price of its altruistic act.[7]

The manner in which kin selection might work is most clearly illustrated by the social insects. For example, termite soldiers often lose their lives defending their colony. But in doing so, they protect the colony, including the king and queen (their parents), and their own genes are increased in the gene pool by the survival of their parents and nieces and nephews to reproduce. In fact, social insects often share a large proportion of their genes with their siblings and parents, so that the survival of relatives ensures the passage of the altruist's own genes to the next generation.

There is some evidence that the mechanism of kin selection functions among humans. In one study, identical twin children (who share their genes) were more cooperative and less competitive during their social interactions than were fraternal twins (who share no more genes than the average siblings).[8] Moreover, relatives are expected to help more than nonrelatives and are helped more than most other persons.[9] In fact, adults' reported willingness to engage in a variety of prosocial behaviors such as making loans, giving large gifts, or helping in the face of danger is highly related to the degree of blood relatedness.[10]

The notion of kin selection, however, does not explain why we assist nonrelatives. People's willingness to assist spouses can be explained in terms of their role as a reproduction resource. But to account for the fact that humans often help nonrelatives, other theoretical mechanisms have been proposed. For example, the genetic similarity theory claims that humans are genetically biased to like and to assist others who are similar to themselves.[11] People who are physically similar to us are particularly likely to share genes; thus, by helping similar others, we increase the probability of their reproducing genes like our own.

Other biologists have attempted to explain the helping of nonrelatives through *reciprocal altruism*.[12] The basic idea is that organisms that assist others may risk their own well-being and their reproductive potential by doing so, but this risk is compensated by the likelihood that the recipient of the prosocial act will reciprocate at a later time. Thus, those who are prosocial increase their chances of survival over those who are not prosocial. For example, a female bluebird who helps a male to raise his motherless young may increase her chances of mating with the male and raising her own young at a later time.[13]

There is considerable debate about the evolutionary bases of human social behavior, including altruism.[14] But regardless of the mechanism used to explain human prosocial behavior, there is reason to believe that humans are genetically predisposed to engage in some prosocial behavior. The very fact that we sympathize with others and help other people demonstrates that we have the biological potential. It is difficult to explain in purely genetic terms why some people are more altruistic than others. However, pursuing every possible explanation for individual differences is important if we wish to know how to foster prosocial tendencies.

GENETICS AND INDIVIDUAL DIFFERENCES IN PROSOCIAL BEHAVIOR

The limited data available on the subject are consistent with the view that genetic factors do play some role in individual differences in prosocial behavior.

As is common in research concerning the role of heredity in social or cognitive functioning, many researchers interested in the genetic basis of altruism have conducted twin studies, examining various indexes of prosocial functioning for both identical twins and fraternal twins. In the most comprehensive study of this type, J. P. Rushton and his colleagues administered self-report questionnaires measuring prosocial behavior, nurturance, aggressiveness, and empathy to 296 pairs of identical adult twins and 179 sets of fraternal, same-sex twins.[15] Having found that the degree of similarity between twins on each measure was considerably higher for identical than for fraternal twins, they concluded that genetic factors accounted for approximately half of the variability in participants' scores. Similarly, in a smaller twin study, researchers found that identical twins were more similar than fraternal twins in their reported empathy (which may be the basis of much altruism; see Chapter 4).[16]

It is difficult to draw firm conclusions from these data, because they were drawn from participants' self-reports, which commonly show greater similarity between identical twins than between fraternal twins.[17] It is possible that the high degree of similarity between identical twins in their reports stems merely from genetically based personality traits such as the need to impress others or to behave in a socially desirable manner—features that are commonly acknowledged as potentially distorting factors in self-report questionnaires. More research, using different instruments, is essential before we can draw any firm conclusions about the role of genetic factors in prosocial behavior. Such methods could involve observations of behavior or reports of prosocial behavior from parents, peers, or other people besides the subjects in the study. In addition, the statistic used to estimate the degree to which genetics contribute to a characteristic varies with the degree of similarity in environments. For example, the influence of the environment is likely to be underestimated if twins live in the same home. Therefore, before drawing firm conclusions, researchers need to investigate the degree to which genetic factors contribute to differences in the prosocial behavior of people who come from very different environments.

Even if genetic factors do play a sizable role in individual differences in prosocial tendencies, environmental factors are also undoubtedly a major influence. Even biologists such as Wilson have acknowledged the role of cultural factors and other environmental influences in the development of prosocial behavior.[18] As we shall see in the next chapters, children learn much about sharing, helping, and comforting activities from their social world.

6/ Cultural Influences

The effect of the social environment on the development of children's social behavior is multifaceted; it can occur simultaneously on different levels, ranging from the parents' specific childrearing practices to the values and beliefs promoted by the culture at large. This chapter examines several cultural and subcultural influences that appear to shape individual differences in prosocial functioning.

CULTURES OF HATE, RIVALRY, AND DISTRUST

THE IK

The Ik are mountain people of Uganda who were studied and described by the anthropologist Colin Turnbull. This small group of hunters had an established social order with laws, rules, and customs until they were deprived of their hunting grounds and subjected to great poverty as a result of political and technological changes. Then the fabric of their society unraveled, and they became people without laws and customs—the "loveless people." In their struggle merely to survive, acrimony, envy, and suspicion reigned. The people cared only about individual survival, and lying, stealing, scheming, cruelty, and even murder became aspects of everyday life. Caring, generosity, and compassion were seen as weakness, and the people generally would not even assist their spouses, parents, or children. Indeed, sons would steal food from their elderly and sick parents and starve them to death.

> In this curious society . . . there is one common value, apart from language, to which all Ik hold tenaciously. It is *ngag*, "food" . . . It is the one standard by which they measure right and wrong, goodness and badness. The very word for "good," *marang*, is defined in terms of food. "Goodness," *marangik*, is defined simply as "food," or, if you press, this will be clarified as "the possession of food," and still further clarified as "*individual* possession of food." Then if you try the word as an adjective and attempt to discover what their concept is of a "good man," *iakw anamarang*, hoping that the answer will be that a good man is a man who helps you fill your own stomach, you get the truly Icien answer: a good man is one who *has* a full stomach. There is goodness in being, but none in doing, at least not in doing to others.[1]

For the Ik, the disintegration of their means of economic survival resulted in the disintegration of their society, their family structure, and their basic value system. "The Ik appear to have disposed of virtually all the qualities that we normally consider are just those qualities that differentiate us from other primates."[2]

THE ALORESE

Another, less extreme example is the Alorese, a group of farmers and hunters who live on an island east of Java and who are sometimes exposed to economic hardships. In 1975 Ronald Rohner described the Alorese in the following manner:

The Alorese are hostile and aggressive. Even though violent outbursts among men are strongly discouraged by the promise of retaliation, and insults are controlled by the prospect of fines, many outlets for hostility exist. Some of these are open to everyone, including women and children. Others are more restricted. Teasing, frightening, ridiculing, and deceiving both children and helpless adults are widespread activities: mothers tease children who are being weaned by nursing neighbors' babies; people ridicule little children's mistakes in speaking; for amusement, little boys are poked in the belly and crotch; children are sent on sham errands for rewards no one intends to give; lies are told to frighten those naive enough to believe them . . . Husbands beat their wives; adults and older children slap younger kin or strike them with weapons.[3]

According to Rohner, the Alorese are limited in their capacity to form strong or enduring emotional attachments, and they approach human relatives with greed, cunning, fear, and defensiveness.[4] And Abram Kardiner said of them, "The personality is devoid of enterprise, is filled with repressed hatred and free-floating aggression over which constant vigilance must be exercised. Cooperation must be at a low level and tenuous social cohesion can be achieved only by dominance-submission attitudes, not by affection and mutual trust."[5]

THE KWAKIUTL

Economic deprivation is not necessary for cruelty to be valued in a culture. Among the traditional cultures described by Ruth Benedict was that of the Kwakiutl, who lived along a narrow strip of the Pacific coast from Alaska to the Puget Sound. According to Benedict, "their civilization was built upon an ample supply of goods, inexhaustible, and obtained without excessive expenditure of labour. The fish, upon which they depended for food, could be taken out of the sea in great hauls."[6]

However, the Kwakiutl of Vancouver Island, whose culture is now lost, valued superiority over others above all else. To achieve this superiority, one had to shame others. Wealth and property, and control of wealth, also were very important goals, because wealth meant power over others and the ability to shame them.

> The object of all Kwakiutl enterprise was to show oneself superior to one's rivals. This will to superiority they exhibited in the most uninhibited fashion. It found expression in uncensored self-glorification and ridicule of all comers . . . All the motivations they recognized centered around the will to superiority. Their social organization, their economic institutions, their religion, birth and death, were all channels for its expression. As they understood triumph, it involved ridicule and scorn heaped publicly upon one's opponents.[7]

Avoidance of ridicule was also a strong motive among the Kwakiutl. "They recognized only one gamut of emotion, that which swings between victory and shame." All of life was viewed through the lens of avoiding shame. For example, if a man was injured in an accident, he was not an object of sympathy, but of shame. Similarly, the death of a relative was seen as a major source of shame. To deal with this shame, people sometimes would head-hunt or kill someone else, someone who had nothing to do with the death. According to Ruth Benedict, "The head-hunting was called 'killing to wipe one's eyes,' and it was a means of getting even by making another household mourn instead."[8]

Although the Kwakiutl were not as brutal and uncaring as the Ik, their culture was dominated by values—superiority, rivalry, and extreme materialism—that are antithetical to positive values such as caring, sharing, and helping others. From descriptions of this culture, we would have to conclude that prosocial values were of little importance to the Kwakiutl.

PROSOCIAL CULTURES

Several traditional societies in various parts of the world (many of which are dying), as well as some more modern examples, provide a sharp contrast to the Ik and Kwakiutl cultures. Among these are the traditional societies of the Polynesian people on the island of Aitutaki, the Maisin and the Arapesh in Papua New Guinea, the Papago and the Hopi Indians in Arizona, and the kibbutz subculture in modern Israel, all of which have been described as harmonious, cooperative, and prosocial.[9]

THE AITUTAKI, MAISIN AND PAPAGO

Nancy and Theodore Graves, who studied the Aitutaki way of life in the 1970s, described it as follows:

Children from traditional families appear to have a strong group orientation from infancy, which is continuously reinforced in dozens of ways: They are raised in large families by a variety of caretakers; they attend and participate in most family and community affairs; they are sent with food or goods to share with other people; they take the family's contribution to the front of the church on Sunday . . . This high degree of group participation and identification and the many manifestations of prosocial behavior that flow from it, we came to recognize, has its roots in the economic, social, and psychological interdependencies fostered by their subsistence economy.[10]

In the traditional culture, Aitutaki children are encouraged from an early age to be oriented toward others and, as a consequence, are quite prosocial in their behavior. They tend to share and cooperate; because people are seen as economically, socially, and psychologically interdependent, assisting others is good for everyone, including oneself.[11]

Similarly, among the traditional Maisin in Papua New Guinea,

> individuals must cooperate with each other in order to survive. Good interpersonal relationships are necessary and of great importance to the Maisin villagers. They believe that the best way to maintain good relations with others is to help them, always when asked for help, and even when there is no request for assistance. Children are taught early to help and to be aware of others' needs.[12]

And Rohner has described the Papago in Arizona as a cooperative, considerate, and warm people: "Major values for a smooth-running Papago social system include work, cooperation, and the avoidance of aggression. The mutual sharing of family work stresses the subordination of self-gratification to close cooperation within the group." Peacefulness is more important than industry (which also is valued), and relationships among tribal members are very warm and supportive.[13]

THE TRADITIONAL HOPI

For the traditional Hopi in Arizona, all aspects of the universe, human and natural, are interdependent. Therefore, cooperation among members of the tribe is considered essential for survival. From very early in life, children are taught that nothing is more important than having a "good heart," that is, feeling trust, respect, and concern for others' rights, welfare, and feelings and seeking harmony within oneself and with others.

> The ideal man . . . remains "Hopi"—peaceful, good, happy, strong, self-controlled, intelligent, wise, and

physically powerful. Poised and tranquil, he keeps a "good heart," concentrates on good thoughts, and avoids anxiety. In his social relationships he stays peaceful, modest, cooperative, unselfish, and law-abiding. All opposite, deviant tendencies are lumped in the concept *kahopi*, and are personified in the evil "two-heart," or witch.[14]

Family interactions are governed by this focus on the group. In the family and in the society, cooperativeness, helpfulness, industriousness, compliance, and nonaggressiveness are encouraged.[15]

THE KIBBUTZ

Even in more contemporary societies there are subcultures in which cooperation and prosocial behavior are unusually valued. One example is the Israeli kibbutz, a communal group that emerged in this century. In the kibbutz, the group

can survive only if the members . . . are highly motivated to work for the welfare of the entire society. The Sabras [native-born Israelis] seem to have acquired this drive. They have learned . . . that prestige is attained primarily by behavior which benefits others. For the youngest children, who are in the process of learning the cultural norms, the most frequent response to the question [What are the things you could do for which others would praise you?] is "generosity" with either assistance or goods. For the oldest group [of children questioned], which presumably has already learned the cultural norms, the most frequent category of response is "social responsibility," i.e., doing those things from which the group as a whole will benefit.[16]

Although some kibbutzim have become somewhat less communal in regard to the living situation of children and some personal property, cooperation and helpfulness remain part of the kibbutz value system.

CULTURAL AND SUBCULTURAL DIFFERENCES IN COOPERATIVE
BEHAVIOR

Differences across subcultures and cultures are also evident in recent studies of cooperative behavior among children. In a series of studies, investigators have examined whether children from various cultural backgrounds compete or cooperate in situations involving peers. For example, Millard Madsen and his colleagues developed a game involving a "cooperation board."[17] Four children play at a time. Each controls a string attached at one end to a corner of the 18-inch-square board and at the other to a holder for a ballpoint pen. The pen makes marks on a sheet of paper attached to the board. The object is to draw lines through circles that are drawn on each of the four sides of the board. But the strings are attached in such a way that a child can pull the pen in only one direction—toward himself or herself. Consequently, it is impossible to draw a line across a circle if another child chooses to pull the string toward himself or herself. If children are to cross the circles and win prizes for doing so, they must cooperate.

The rules of the game can be varied to promote either cooperation or competition. For example, telling the children that all of them will receive prizes if they cross all four circles in a set length of time generally heightens cooperation, regardless of the children's background. In contrast, assigning a circle to each child and telling the children that they will get prizes only if they cross their own circle often heighten competition. Even in this case, however, cooperation remains the best strategy because no one can win if the children compete.

Another procedure that has been used to study cross-cultural differences in cooperation, rivalry, and competition is a reward allocation task. Children are presented with a series of cards in which they must choose between two alternatives, such as keeping three pennies for themselves while a peer receives four pennies versus choosing a card indicating that both the child and the peer will receive three pennies. There are several variations of this game, but in general they can be used to assess whether the children are motivated to be superior (maximize their own gain relative to the other) or generous (maximize the other's gain in absolute terms) or to maximize one's own rewards, regardless of the outcome for the peer.[18]

Using methods of this sort, researchers have found some interesting differences in the behavior of children from different cultures and subcultures.[19] For example, children from all cultures seem to cooperate on the cooperation board when they are told that the rewards are to be shared by the group rather than won by individuals. However, when children are told that rewards are individual (that is, that each child has his or her own circle, and gets a prize only when it is crossed), children reared in traditional rural subcultures and traditional, semiagricultural settlements cooperate more than do children reared in modern, urban settings. Children from urban settings often pull on the strings so hard that the strings break and no one wins. Specifically, in games of the sort described above, children in small Mexican communities are far less competitive and avoid conflict more than urban middle-class Mexicans, Mexican-American, Afro-American, or Anglo-American children.[20] Children from kibbutzim and small Arab villages in Israel cooperate more than urban Israeli children.[21] Similar differences have been found for Colombian children and Korean children.[22] In addition, children from American and European backgrounds are less cooperative than children from semitraditional cultures in Kenya, children of Aboriginal Australian heritage, and children from New Zealand Maori traditional rural cultures.[23] Even children from urban non-

European settings such as Japan and Zambia tend to be competitive and rivalrous when playing games such as those described above.[24]

The strong effect of culture on children's cooperation, competition, and rivalrous behavior is demonstrated in studies of children from traditional cultures who are exposed to the influence of modern urban societies. Children who are in the process of assimilating or are exposed to the dominant, urban culture in their school tend to be less cooperative than children from the same cultural group with less exposure to the urban culture. For example, Australian Aborigines who live in a traditional manner tend to be more cooperative than Aborigines with higher educational goals and a stronger orientation to the European culture.[25] Similarly, although Canadian Indians (particularly males) are more cooperative than urban Canadians, those attending a school with Caucasian children are more competitive than more traditionally reared Indian children.[26] Similar differences have been found between traditional Aitutaki children and those attending westernized schools.[27]

Even if some accounts of traditional cultures have been exaggerated or some of the customs have been misunderstood because of the writer's Western perspective, it is clear that cultures differ in the degree to which they value prosocial traits and behaviors rather than aggressiveness, rivalry, and brutality. Consequently, questions arise concerning the mechanisms in various cultures that produce the differences in observed prosocial and antisocial values and behaviors.

SOURCES OF CULTURAL VARIATION

Psychologists, sociologists, and anthropologists have offered a variety of explanations for the differences among cultures in typical levels of cooperation and prosocial behavior. Most of the explanations have to do with the socialization practices and values passed from generation to generation. Often the explanations are informed speculations offered by an investigator who has observed one specific culture. Unfortunately, few researchers have systematically compared the socialization of children in more than one culture in an attempt to identify factors that contribute to cultural differences in perceptions of ideal character and the valuing of cooperation and prosocial values in contrast to aggressive, hostile, and rivalrous behavior. Nonetheless, observations of cooperative and competitive behavior, aggression, hostility, and prosocial tendencies in nonwestern cultures are useful in understanding how culture may influence the development of prosocial and antisocial tendencies.

WARMTH AND AFFECTION

Some investigators have hypothesized that differences in the degree to which children experience love rather than rejection from caregivers influences their basic character and attitudes toward other human beings. For example, Rohner argued that personality differences between the Papago and Alorese reflect differences in parenting behaviors: Papago parents are warm, supportive, and nurturant, whereas the Alorese are hostile, neglectful, and rarely warm. According to Rohner, Papago adults want children very much, and children of either sex are welcomed and treated with love. Relatives fondle and make much of children, and parents dislike being separated from their children.

> Babies are swung gently in hammocks, watched, picked up and talked to whenever they cry or whenever the mother is not busy. A baby is usually within sight of his mother . . . Mothers are constantly and

warmly concerned with their babies, and babies are never neglected.

Mothers who are weaning their children try to avoid tears. Rather than enforcing strict, abrupt weaning, they either distract the child's attention whenever he attempts to nurse or leave him with one of his grandmothers for gradually increasing periods of time . . .

Everything that a child cries for he may play with. An adult may protect his belongings by hiding them, by trying to distract the child, or by providing a substitute, but if the child insists, the treasure will be delivered.[28]

The Papago rarely use corporal punishment unless they have had contact with Caucasian families who spank their children.

Some demands start to be made on children when they are about 4. The children start to learn the skills they will need. In training children, adults give a great deal of instruction "not in *how* to do things but in *why* they should be done."[29] However, children who are slow to work are not coerced or strongly condemned, because they are still merely children. In addition, they are given much freedom of choice in matters such as going to school, eating, or receiving medical care. Children are pressured primarily in regard to their responsibilities to the group, although children who do not live up to adults' expectations are merely lectured, scolded, and threatened with supernatural actions. Parents do not withdraw their love from or use sharp derision with their children.

In contrast, among the Alorese the recognition associated with parenthood is greater for men than for women, so women often resent bearing children. Although the newborn is held, fondled, and played with, this indulgence does not last long; when the infant is about 2 weeks old, the mother returns to work in the fields. From that time on, the infant's care is inconsistent, and provision of food may be unreliable.

> Alorese children have no stable or dependable source of care and affection. Young children live in an insecure world, where need-satisfaction is unpredictable and becomes available mainly through their own manipulations. Even with regard to food, young children are left without any assured provisions. Throughout the day they must rely on the handouts they can get by begging or screaming at older children and adults.[30]

As children grow, they face teasing, lying, deception, and other forms of mild aggression. For example, during weaning children are pushed away from the breast and slapped; sometimes they are sent to live with relatives. After weaning, mothers may tease their children by taking neighbors' babies to their breasts. For amusement, older children and adults poke, prod, ridicule, and frighten young children. For example, adults may flash a knife and threaten to cut off a child's ear. Mothers often ignore or punish their children when they react badly to separations. Children and adolescents gain and lose property at the whim of adults. Rohner concluded that among the Alorese, "parental behavior is characterized by continual neglect, only occasional warmth, and frequent aggression in the form of deceit, teasing, ridicule, and frightening children—often for the sole purpose of amusement . . . Parental rejection in the forms of both neglect and aggression is conspicuous."[31] He further suggested that such parental rejection was the cause of the hostile, distrustful, and often aggressive behavior of the Alorese, whereas the nurturing, supportive parenting of the Papago contributed to the cooperative, peaceful Papago personality.

Other social scientists have come to conclusions similar to Rohner's. For example, Margaret Mead described a New Guinea tribe called the Arapesh who were gentle, cooperative, loving, generous, and highly responsive to the needs and feelings of other people.[32] Mead hypothesized that the personality of the Arapesh was a result of the tender attention and caring that parents gave their children.

Thus the cross-cultural literature is consistent with the idea that warm, supportive parenting may provide the foundation for caring, prosocial behavior and character. This perspective is consistent with the views of many modern psychologists such as Erik Erikson, Mary Ainsworth, and Alan Sroufe, although it appears that parental warmth alone may not be sufficient for the development of prosocial tendencies (see Chapter 7).[33]

INCULCATION OF CULTURAL VALUES

A related explanation for cultural differences in prosocial and aggressive tendencies concerns the degree to which various cultures specifically teach and reinforce positive and negative values and behaviors.

For example, Rohner reported that Papago children often are lectured in the evenings by fathers and grandfathers on the importance of industry, honest, and peacefulness.[34] Nonaggressiveness and cooperation are also actively encouraged by the traditional Hopi people.[35] Similarly, in the Israeli kibbutzim, parents and teachers teach cooperative values and discourage competition among children. Parents in the kibbutz have reported that generosity and cooperation are the most frequently rewarded behaviors, whereas selfishness and failure to cooperative are among those most frequently punished.

The formal teaching methods in the kibbutz are also noted for their minimal emphasis on competitive goals and techniques. Grades and examinations are viewed as unnecessary or even undesirable. Competition, with all its punitive aspects, is far less intense in the classroom of the kibbutz than in that of the city. Not only do the agents of socialization avoid inducing a favorable set toward competition . . . Generally, kibbutz children do not accept competition as a socially desirable norm and dislike those who try to excel over members of their own group. This anti-competition attitude is so strong that, according to some teachers, students are ashamed of being consistently at the top of the class.[36]

Another example of a modern society in which cooperative values were specifically taught is the Soviet Union. Urie Bronfenbrenner, who studied childrearing methods there in the 1960s, reported that children were (and still may be) taught and reinforced for behavior that directed at bettering the position of the group or collective: "From the very beginning stress is placed on teaching children to share and to engage in joint activity. Frequent reference is made to common ownership: "moe eto nashe; nashe moe" [mine is ours; ours is mine]. Collective play is emphasized. Not only group games, but special complex toys are designed which require the cooperation of two or three children to make them work."[37]

Clearly, in some cultures prosocial and cooperative values have been purposefully taught and reinforced. However, cooperative, prosocial values and behaviors may also be learned without purposeful teaching of them.

THE STRUCTURE OF THE CULTURE AND EVERYDAY LIFE

Cooperation and prosocial behaviors may be learned from the structure of society in which people live. In many traditional cultures, where the survival of the group depends on cooperation and helping among kin and neighbors, the child's everyday experiences and chores involve cooperation and prosocial actions because they are part of the routine of everyday life.

For example, the dramatic differences in the level of cooperativeness of rural and urban Mexican children may reflect different patterns of family functioning in the two settings.[38] In poor agricultural communities, people must cooperate with family members merely to obtain enough food to survive. Because cooperation is essential to the family's existence, it is expected; in addition, from an early age, children cooperate with others in tasks such as childrearing, fetching water, and obtaining food.

A recognition of the importance of cooperation for survival in nonwestern, traditional rural cultures is epitomized by a saying of the traditional Aitutaki. If a fisherman caught more fish than his family could use that day, he would "store the surplus in his neighbor's belly." Then he and his family could expect a constant supply of fresh fish through gifts from his neighbors. In this manner, "a network of mutual obligation, caring, and concern is formed throughout the village."[39]

In contrast, in Western urban settings, children frequently are encouraged to do better than their peers and to do their homework alone. Test scores and college entrance tests tend to be based on the individual child's performance relative to the performance of peers. In fact, success in urban settings (especially in capitalistic societies) often depends on individual achievement and competition; family survival rarely depends on children's contributions to the family, and children seldom perform chores that make important contributions to the well-being of the family.

In a fascinating study, Beatrice and John Whiting examined the activities of children from six cultures and found that certain facets of daily life and behavior were associated with differences across the cultures in the children's performance of prosocial and socially responsible behaviors.[40] The children, aged 3 to 11 years, were observed in a variety of normal social interactions: at home, in the fields, at school, during play and work. Every interaction was recorded and classified. One important dimension of the children's behavior was *altruism versus egoistic behavior*. Altruistic behaviors were actions that benefited others such as "offers help" (including food, toys, and helpful information), "offers support," and "suggests responsibly" (makes helpful suggestions). The egoistic end of the dimension included behaviors such as "seeks dominance," "seeks attention," and "seeks help"—behaviors that benefit the actor rather than other people.

Most of the children in three cultures—Kenyan, Mexican, and Filipino—scored high in altruism. In contrast, children from communities in India, Okinawa, and New England (in the United States) generally scored relatively low in altruism and high in egoism. To examine the possible sources of this difference, Whiting and Whiting compared the three cultures in which altruism was high with the three in which it was low. In the cultures in which the children tended to be prosocial, children were assigned and performed more duties that were important to the family's economic security and the welfare of other family members; for example, girls took care of their younger sisters and brothers, and boys helped tend the herds. Such contributions to the family's welfare as assisting with obtaining food, carrying water, cooking, and caring for animals and younger siblings are rather obvious, even to young children. Thus, the children learned from an early age that they must be responsible to their family and that their contributions to the family were important.[41]

In addition, in the prosocial cultures, people tended to live in extended families and women made significant contributions to the economic well-being of the family, including the food supply. Conversely, in the cultures in which children tended to be less prosocial, people tended to live in nuclear families, and the organization of the society was more complex: occupations tended to be specialized, governments were centralized, and there was a class or caste system. According to Whiting and Whiting,

> in the simpler, kin-oriented societies, with economies based upon subsistence gardening, altruistic behavior is highly valued and individual egoistic achievement frowned upon. Women must work in the fields, and the children must help in order for the family to subsist. To offer help, to support others, and to be responsible are taught both by precept and practice. Being helplessly dependent, showing off, boasting, and being egoistically dominant are incompatible with such a way of life.
>
> On the other hand, in the more complex societies, where no child knows what he is going to be when he grows up, individual achievement and success must be positively valued. To help a friend sitting next to you in an examination is defined as cheating.[42]

Using methods somewhat similar to those of Whiting and Whiting, Graves and Graves observed patterns of social interaction among the Aitutaki.[43] Consistent with the Whitings' findings, Aitutaki children who lived in urban settings were less prosocial and performed fewer chores than did children raised in traditional extended families.

The ways in which Western technology can undermine traditional values are exemplified by the effect of technology on the traditions of the Aitutaki. The introduction of electricity brought freezers, with the result that people in each household could freeze fish and did not need to depend on their neighbors. Similarly, the introduction of sheet metal roofing eliminated the periodic need for communal thatching parties; the availability of rented tractors reduced the need for the exchange of labor among members of the community; and the availability of outboard motors reduced the need for communal fishing. As a consequence, "People can now 'afford' to quarrel with their neighbors, and the social skills that had developed to prevent, deflect, or resolve such quarrels atrophy or are never learned."[44] Western technology and the job specialization associated with urban societies simply decrease the need and often even the desirability of cooperative and prosocial behavior.

From the cross-cultural data, it seems apparent that there are differences among cultures in cooperative and prosocial behavior. These differences seem to be associated with differences in the degree to which children are supported and nurtured, are assigned chores that significantly contribute to the well-being of the family, and are taught cultural values. In addition, the structure of traditional, nonurban, subsistence cultures seems to promote a cooperative orientation.

An important possible limitation of these findings is the fact that in the cooperative, prosocial groups studied, positive behavior is typically directed toward members of one's own kinship group or neighbors. Cooperative or helping behavior in such cultures may be motivated primarily by a desire for approval from family, friends, and neighbors and by a recognition that positive actions directed toward people who are known are likely to result in mutual benefit (as in communal fishing ventures) or reciprocity on future occasions (as with the fish stored in the Aitutaki's neighbor's belly).

Thus, it is not clear that children in traditional societies are actually more altruistic (that is, sympathetic and other-oriented) in their *motives* for their behaviors; nor is it clear whether they are more prosocial toward strangers than are children in industrialized societies.

Although the cross-cultural research is quite informative about the ways in which socialization can affect the development of prosocial and cooperative behavior, few cross-cultural studies have carefully measured and analyzed actual childrearing practices. Thus, to learn more about the socialization of prosocial behaviors, we must turn to research conducted in a single society.

7 / Socialization in the Family

As we have seen, cultural differences in the structure and functioning of the family are associated with differences in the frequency with which children perform prosocial behaviors. Many cultural values regarding what is considered acceptable and unacceptable behavior are passed down from one generation to another within the family and the larger society. However, there are also large differences *within* cultures in the degree to which children share, help, or comfort others, in their cooperativeness and competitiveness, and in their concern for the well-being of other people. These differences within cultures may stem from a number of factors, including biological predispositions, the economic situation of the family, and the child's level of understanding of others' emotions. Perhaps the most obvious influence on the child's prosocial development is the family.

An excellent example of how parents can influence the development of prosocial tendencies is found in Samuel and Pearl Oliner's book *The Altruistic Personality*.[1] The Oliners studied people in Europe who either did or did not help Jews to escape from Nazi oppression during World War II. To provide such help in a country controlled by Germany during the war could cost the helper his or her life and the lives of loved ones. Why did some people help at great risk to themselves when so many other people did not?

The Oliners interviewed rescuers and nonrescuers to try to answer this question. They found that an important factor that differentiated rescuers from people who did not assist was the values that were expressed in their parents' verbalizations and actual behavior. Values of equity—notions of fair procedures, fair allocation of goods, impartial administration of justice—were emphasized in many of the homes of both rescuers and nonrescuers. However, rescuers were more likely than nonrescuers to say that they learned generosity and caring from their parents or another most influential person. Here are examples of their reports:

> My mother was a model of Christian faith and love of neighbor.

> I learned generosity, to be open, to help people.

> I learned to be good to one's neighbor, honesty, scruples—to be responsible, concerned, and considerate. To work—and work hard. But also to help—to the point of leaving one's work to help one's neighbor.

> To be good and caring, to love people. Mother always said to remember to do some good for someone at least once a day.[2]

When recalling the values that they had learned from parents or the most influential person in their life, 44 percent of rescuers mentioned caring or generosity, whereas only 21 percent of bystanders did so.

In addition to learning to care for others, rescuers learned to be more inclusive than did bystanders in regard to the groups to which they felt ethical obligations. Nonrescuers tended to report that their parents emphasized ethical obligations to family, friends, elders, the church, and country, but not other groups of people: "My father taught me to work hard and not to tell lies—to be neighborly and polite to elders—to go to church and to be a good Catholic—to be good to your family." In contrast, 39 percent of rescuers, in comparison to 13 percent of bystanders, reported that their parents emphasized that ethical values were to apply to all human beings:

They taught me to respect all human beings.

They taught me to respect a man no matter what his origin.

He taught me to love my neighbor—to consider him my equal whatever his nationality or religion. He taught me especially to be tolerant.[3]

This training at home was reflected in the reasons that rescuers gave for their helping activities. Approximately half of all rescuers reported that a universalistic obligation was at least one reason for their helping, and the reports of the Jewish survivors in this regard were consistent with those of the rescuers. For example, one rescuer reported the following reason for his or her behavior: "The reason is that every man is equal. We all have the right to live. It was plain murder, and I couldn't stand that. I would help a Mohammedan just as well as a Jew. We have got to live as humans and not as beasts. They [the Nazis] were worse than beasts."[4]

However, sympathy and caring were the most common reasons for helping mentioned by both rescuers and rescued survivors:

I was just sorry for them.

I did it out of sympathy and kindness.

I did it out of a feeling of compassion for those who were weaker and who needed help.[5]

Indeed, the Oliners found that the rescuers scored higher than bystanders on a self-report measure of their tendency to be moved by the emotions of others.

Parents of rescuers and bystanders differed in more ways than in their emphasis on caring and in applying ethical principles universally. For example, parents of rescuers used less physical punishment and more reasoning in their discipline than did parents of nonrescuers, although the groups did not differ in the degree to which they recalled being disciplined for disobedience and negative behaviors such as aggression, lying, or stealing. Moreover, more nonrescuers perceived that parental punishment had been routine and gratuitous—"a cathartic release of aggression on the part of the parent and unrelated to their behavior."[6] Finally, rescuers reported that their families were closer than did bystanders.

Thus, there appeared to be numerous differences in rescuers' and bystanders' socialization histories. Parents of rescuers, more than parents of bystanders, tended to emphasize caring and the application of ethical obligations to all people, reasoned with their children in disciplinary encounters, and used relatively little physical punishment. Parents of rescuers also modeled caring behavior in their interactions with people outside the family, as well as in the way in which they administered discipline and punishment. In addition, rescuers had closer relations to their parents than did bystanders, a finding that suggests that parents of rescuers were relatively warm and supportive.

CHILDREARING PRACTICES

The Oliners' findings on the socialization of rescuers and nonrescuers mirror research findings on the socialization of children's prosocial behavior in everyday life.

Parental modeling, communication of values and caring, and disciplinary techniques all appear to be associated with the development of children's prosocial behavior. In addition, the child's emotional relationship with his or her family—especially the nature of the relationship with caregivers—seems to influence the child's capacity for caring and the effectiveness of parental disciplinary practices.

MODELING

Children imitate the behaviors of other people, particularly important, powerful, and nurturant people.[7] It is not entirely clear why they do. Perhaps children identify with significant people in their environment and want to be like them; perhaps they want to behave in a socially appropriate, competent manner and believe that adults' behaviors are good exemplars. In addition, children may be rewarded for imitating adults or may believe that they will obtain the material objects and power of adults if they are like them. Furthermore, children may learn new behaviors by imitating models.[8] In any case, children do tend to copy the moral, or immoral, behaviors of parents, as well as those of peers and other adults.

A considerable amount of research supports this assertion. Much of the research involves analogue studies conducted in experimental laboratories that simulate events that happen in real life. In the analogue studies, an adult, usually someone the child has just met, models a given behavior, and then the child's imitation of that behavior is observed. It is assumed that the adult model is analogous to the models provided by parents in the home.

In studies of the effects of modeling on children's prosocial behavior, a child and an adult typically play a game in which they earn prizes, money, or tokens that can be traded for prizes. The adult model then donates some or all of his or her earnings to some needy person or group—for example, poor children or children who have no opportunity to earn prizes. With some children, the model may choose not to donate. Then the child may be left alone, and his or her donating behavior monitored. In general, researchers have found that children imitate the prosocial or selfish behavior modeled by the adult.[9]

The findings of nonexperimental studies generally are consistent with those from laboratory studies. For example, Carolyn Zahn-Waxler, Marian Radke-Yarrow, and Robert King found that mothers' empathic, warm caretaking (which, by definition, involves the modeling of prosocial behavior) was associated with 1- to 2-year-olds' prosocial behaviors directed toward others in distress.[10] Similarly, preschool boys who represented their fathers as models of generosity and compassion in doll play shared more than did boys who did not view their fathers in this way.[11]

In addition, in a study of Freedom Riders—people who were involved in civil rights activities in the South in the 1960s, often at risk to themselves—the activists who were most fully committed in terms of time and effort reported having parents who explicitly modeled altruistic behavior. For example,

One of the Fully Committed reported that "my father carried me on his shoulders during the Sacco-Vanzetti parades"; another described how his father fought on the side of the Loyalists in the Spanish Civil War; a third described how his mother "felt close to Jesus and warmed by His teachings. She devoted her entire life to Christian education." Finally, another respondent's father was outraged by the Nazi atrocities and, though

> overage and apparently disqualified on grounds of
> health, was finally accepted into the military during the
> Second World War. In short, we seem to have found the
> presence of altruistic models in the backgrounds of Fully
> Committed altruists, models whose very behavior ap-
> parently influenced the course of their offspring's
> activities.[12]

Similarly, in another study of rescuers of Jews in World
War II, rescuers tended to strongly identify with a parent who held firm opinions on moral issues and on
serving as a model of moral conduct.[13]

In general, consistent with the findings in the Oliners'
study, adults' modeling of altruism seems to have a
greater influence on children's behavior if there is a close
bond between the adult and the child. In the study of
the civil rights workers, the most committed, altruistic
workers reported not only that their parents were models of altruism, but also that they had warm, cordial,
and respecting relationships with one or both parents.[14]

Similar results have been obtained in regard to less
dramatic real-life helping activities such as volunteering
for a telephone crisis-counseling agency. Volunteers
who engaged in more sustained altruistic activity—that
is, finished the 6-month work commitment that they
had made when they were trained—tended to have
good relationships with their parents and viewed their
parents as modeling altruism. In contrast, those with
relatively poor relationships with their parents and who
reported relatively low levels of parental altruism finished their commitment primarily if the group with
which they trained was cohesive; those who did not like
their training group tended not to finish. Apparently,
people who did not report warm relationships with their
parents yet finished their 6-month commitment obtained social rewards for maintaining their association

with the agency and were motivated to continue their relationships with the other people in their training group.[15] These people appeared to continue as volunteers primarily for social, not for altruistic or moral reasons.

Although warm interaction with adults generally seems to enhance the probability that children will imitate the adults' altruistic behavior, adults who treat the child warmly regardless of the child's behavior are not necessarily imitated, especially if the imitated prosocial behavior is costly.[16] Perhaps children interpret such noncontingent warmth from adults as indicating that they can do whatever they please without incurring disapproval. However, in real life, socializers' warmth is seldom noncontingent; all but very permissive parents tend to be less warm when their children misbehave. Thus, in all but permissive homes, parental warmth and support may be expected to enhance the likelihood that children will model parents' prosocial actions.

Although children do not always imitate the moral behaviors of their socializers, it is clear that parental modeling of altruism can have a powerful effect on the altruistic tendencies of children. Children exposed to altruistic caregivers apparently learn prosocial behaviors and frequently seem to adopt the caring orientations of their parents.

THE EFFECTS OF ADULTS' PREACHINGS

Adults also may model prosocial behaviors symbolically—that is, with their words. They may talk about altruistic activities, the importance of helping others, or the desirability of generosity. Such verbalizations appear to have some influence on children's prosocial development.

As the Oliners found in their study, parental preachings about caring and the universality of ethical standards often were reflected in the rescuers' own value systems. Parental modeling of prosocial behavior and their preaching often may go together; the telephone volunteers at the crisis center who reported that their parents modeled altruism and were warm also reported that their parents preached altruism. For example, they reported that their parents "told me I should be willing to lend a helping hand" and "urged me to donate money to charities."[17]

However, the precise content of adults' preachings may influence the degree to which children take those preachings to heart. Children exposed to adults who merely state norms regarding altruism, such as "People should give," are not particularly likely to share.[18] However, when adults talk about the effects of sharing on other people or highlight the needy state of a potential recipient of aid, children's donating often is enhanced. For example, in one study, children were told that poor children "would be so happy and excited if they could buy food and toys. After all, poor children have almost nothing. If everyone would help these children maybe they wouldn't look so sad."[19] Children exposed to this empathy-inducing preaching were particularly likely to donate money to the needy children.

Clearly, socializers can enhance children's sharing with their words as well as their deeds. However, sympathy-inducing preachings appear to be more effective than merely telling children that they should help or share.[20] In addition, socializers who preach altruism but do not model it may have little positive effect on children's prosocial development. In fact, parents who are inconsistent in their message to the child tend to have children who are not particularly altruistic.[21]

INSTRUCTIONS TO HELP

Adults' instructions or directions to help are another type of verbalization that can affect children's prosocial behavior. Direct, constraining instructions (such as "What I'd like you to do is give some of the pennies you win to them each time you win five") increase sharing, more so than permissive instructions (such as "You may give some of the pennies you win to them if you like, but you don't have to") or instructions not to share. Young children instructed to share tend to do so in private, as well as when an adult is near by, and the effects of the instructions may last for weeks. However, the effectiveness of the more directive instructions may decrease somewhat with age during the elementary school years.[22]

Directive instructions may be helpful in promoting prosocial behavior because they induce children to rehearse or practice performing prosocial behaviors. Children who are induced to help others seem to be more prosocial thereafter.[23] For example, elementary school children induced to donate some gift coupons to needy children were more likely a day later to perform a dull task for hospitalized children rather than play with attractive toys.[24]

Such findings are consistent with Whiting and Whiting's finding that children from cultures in which they are routinely assigned responsibilities for others are particularly prosocial (see Chapter 6). Children who have opportunities to help others may learn new helping skills and find that they often feel good when they produce positive outcomes for other people. Moreover, children may be rewarded for engaging in prosocial actions (for example, they may be praised), and this outcome would be expected to increase the likelihood of their assisting in the future. In addition, children who are induced to help others may come to think of themselves as helpful people and, consequently, engage in more prosocial behavior at a later time. However, children are unlikely to think that they themselves really wanted to help if they are forced (rather than induced) to help; this may be why constraining instructions, which give the child little choice, seem to become less effective as children grow older.

PROSOCIAL ATTRIBUTIONS

The attributions or reasons that adults provide for children's prosocial behaviors may also affect whether or not children come to view themselves as helpful people. For example, in one study, 7- and 8-year-olds were brought to a research trailer at their schools three times. On the first occasion the children played a bowling game, earned prizes, and were told that they could donate some of their earnings to poor children. If they did not do so, the experimenter subtly pressured the child to do so with prompts such as "Remember, you can give one of your marbles to the poor children if you want to." Then, after the children donated, some children (the attribution group) were told, "Gee, you shared quite a bit. I guess you're the kind of person who likes to help others whenever you can. Yes, you are a very nice and helpful person." A similar procedure was repeated a week later, when a different adult induced the child to assist her and then said "You know, you certainly are a nice person. I bet you're someone who is helpful whenever possible." Finally 1 to 2 weeks after the second session, a third adult went into the children's classrooms and announced that she was from the local hospital for sick children and was collecting drawings and craft materials (egg cartons, scraps of material) to help cheer up the children there. Each child was given three pieces of paper for drawings and asked to return the pictures in a bag, along with any craft materials, within 2 days. Children who had twice heard the altruistic attributions for their prosocial behavior assisted more than children who received no attributions or children who were given social approval (praise) for helping. Thus, attributing altruistic motivations to children appeared to enhance their prosocial responsiveness.[25]

Providing attributions seems to be a useful procedure for increasing a variety of desirable behaviors (for example, cooperation, self-control, and tidiness) in children.[26] Unfortunately, parents do not seem to be aware of the effectiveness of this strategy and seldom use it.[27]

DISCIPLINE

When children are perceived as doing something wrong or as not behaving as expected (for example, not sharing when asked to do so), parents often discipline their children. There are a variety of approaches that a parent can take. Consider a situation in which a 4-year-old boy refuses to share his blocks with his 2-year-old sister, who then becomes upset and cries. His parents, if they observe this interaction, may do nothing at all; they may scold the boy and send him to his room; or they may come over, roughly pull the boy off the floor, and hit him. Alternatively, the boy's parents may try to talk to him about his behavior; for example, they may say, "Look, you made your sister sad" or "How would you feel if your older brother wouldn't play with you?"

Researchers have found that some disciplinary techniques are more effective than others at promoting prosocial behavior. The techniques most commonly examined have been the use of reasoning and physical punishment.

Inductions. Reasoning in the service of discipline has been labeled induction. Inductions frequently consist of the adult's pointing out the consequences of the child's behavior for other people. ("See, you made her cry") or highlighting another person's emotional state ("Now she feels bad"). Parental use of inductions has often been associated with higher levels of prosocial behavior in children.[28]

Surprisingly, inductions appear to be effective even with very young children. In a very interesting and important study, Zahn-Waxler, Radke-Yarrow, and King studied mothers' reactions to 1- and 2-year-olds' prosocial behaviors and transgressions (that is, the children were the cause of another's psychological or physical distress) over a 9-month period.[29] Some mothers disciplined their children by using emotionally charged explanations such as "Can't you see Al's hurt?" or "You made Doug cry. It's not nice to bite." Their children were more prosocial and more likely to try to make reparation for their transgressions. In contrast, some mothers used unexplained verbal prohibitions such as "Stop that!" Their children exhibited low levels of prosocial behavior and reparation.

Inductions that point out others' feelings and needs may be especially effective in promoting prosocial development. In addition, parental inductions that call attention to the harm done by the child and that encourage the child to make reparation and consider the victim's feelings have been linked with school-age children's consideration and helpfulness.[30]

Inductions may not be equally effective for all children. Prosocial behavior seems to be associated with inductive discipline only if used by mothers who typically do not use punitive (power-assertive) discipline.[31] Inductions also seem to be more useful for children who have had a history of exposure to inductions than for children who have usually been exposed to punitive discipline.[32]

Psychologists have suggested a number of reasons for the effectiveness of inductive discipline. First, by directing their children's attention to other people and others' needs and emotional states, parents encourage their children to take the perspective of other people and to sympathize with them. Techniques that induce children to empathize with others seem to be quite effective in fostering altruism; I return to this issue shortly. Second, inductions provide reasons for behaving, or not behaving, in certain ways—reasons that the child can remember and apply in new situations. Third, parents who use inductive discipline implicitly communicate that the child is responsible for his or her own behavior. Fourth, parents who reason with their children rather than merely yelling at them or hitting them provide a controlled, caring model for imitation. Finally, an optimal learning situation may be created when parents use inductions. Children learn best when they are not overly scared, aroused, or angry. When parents use inductions, children are unlikely to be too emotionally aroused to attend to what the parent says and to the consequences of his or her own behavior.[33]

Power-assertive discipline. Power-assertive discipline includes physical punishment, the deprivation of privileges, or threats of either of these. Parental use of power-assertive, techniques is generally associated with low levels of prosocial behavior or is unrelated to prosocial development.[34]

The effects of power-assertive techniques on children's behavior probably vary with the severity of the discipline and the quality of the parent-child relationship. Excessive use of power-assertive techniques by parents generally is associated with low levels of moral development in children. Similarly, power-assertive discipline administered by cold, punitive parents is unlikely to have positive effects.[35] However, if power assertion is used in a measured and rational way by warm, supportive parents who usually use other forms of discipline, it may not have detrimental effects on the child's prosocial development.[36]

There are several reasons why excessive use of power-assertive discipline may not promote prosocial development. Parents who consistently use power-assertive techniques model aggressive behavior for their children to imitate. In addition, children who are harshly punished will not be motivated to attend to what their parents say or to try to please their parents. Rather, these children will tend to be frightened in disciplinary contexts, and they will focus on their own needs rather than on those of other people. Thus, children who are frequently disciplined with punitive tactics may not learn to empathize with other people, and they may learn that the primary reason for performing behaviors such as helping others is to avoid punishment. Consequently, they will not be motivated to assist others when there is no threat of punishment, and they will not internalize values related to altruism.[37]

REINFORCEMENT

Many parents (and psychologists) believe that an effective way to increase the frequency of desired behaviors, including helping or getting As on report cards, is to reward these behaviors. Thus, parents may indicate their approval of prosocial behaviors by giving their child a treat or a gift. In addition, they may praise their children for performing desired behaviors. In fact, material and social rewards do have short-term effects; for example, children rewarded for sharing tend to share more when given an opportunity to do so shortly after being rewarded.[38]

However, it is unclear if the effects of rewards—especially material rewards—are enduring. In most studies in which material rewards have been associated with an increase in children's prosocial behavior at a later time or in a different situation, reinforcement was used in combination with modeling or other techniques.[39] Social rewards such as praise may have stronger long-term effects on children's prosocial behavior than do material rewards, but this proposition has not been adequately tested.

Under certain circumstances, the provision of material rewards for children's prosocial actions may actually undermine the development of altruism. Children who are frequently rewarded for their prosocial behaviors may come to believe that they assist others primarily to receive rewards.[40] In a study with second- to fifth-graders, some children were told that they would be rewarded for performing a task to help hospitalized children (or saw other children being told that there would be a reward), whereas others were not. In addition, mothers were questioned regarding the degree to which they valued rewards and used them with their children. Children who were told that they would be rewarded for helping assisted more in that context than did children who were not told that they would be rewarded. However, the association of rewards with helping led to less prosocial behavior when the children were given a second, subsequent opportunity to help in a context in which rewards were not mentioned and the children were left alone. But the linking of rewards with helping was detrimental only if the children's mothers valued and used rewards relatively frequently. Moreover, mothers who felt more positive about using rewards reported that their children were relatively low in prosocial behavior. Thus, children who were frequently exposed to rewards in the home seemed to be less intrinsically motivated to help when there were no rewards for doing so.[41] Such findings suggest that providing children with material rewards for their prosocial actions is not an effective way to promote an internalized, altruistic orientation.

QUALITY OF THE PARENT-CHILD RELATIONSHIP

As was discussed previously, children are more likely to imitate a model if the child has a positive relationship with the adult. The primary exception to this pattern is if the adult has displayed noncontingent warmth; then the child seems to do just as he or she pleases.

This same pattern seems to be true in general. Parental warmth and support are weakly associated with children's generosity and helping, whereas high levels of parental permissiveness combined with warmth are not.[42] Whether or not parental nurturance is associated with prosocial behavior in children seems to vary as a function of the other childrearing practices used by the parents. When parents are nurturant and use effective practices such as modeling and inductions, children are likely to be relatively prosocial. If parents are nurturant but do not set high standards, model prosocial behaviors, and use procedures that induce their children to consider others' perspectives, children are less likely to be socially responsible and prosocial.

It is likely that children with nurturant parents feel good about their parents and are receptive to their influence, including their inductions, preachings, and modeling.[43] Thus, the childrearing practices of nurturant parents are likely to be more effective than those of cold, nonsupportive parents. In addition, parents who are supportive tend to have children who are securely attached to them,[44] and securely attached children may be more positively oriented to other people in general.[45] Thus, children with supportive parents may be especially open to empathizing with others and particularly concerned about others. In fact, children who are securely attached at 1 to 2 years of age exhibited more sympathy and prosocial behavior in their preschool classroom than did children with certain types of insecure attachments.[46]

It appears that parental nurturance can foster the development of children's prosocial tendencies, if parents also use other effective childrearing techniques. However, parental nurturance combined with high levels of permissiveness does not appear to encourage the development of altruism.

THE IMPORTANCE OF EMPATHY TRAINING

The importance of promoting sympathy and empathy in the socialization of prosocial behavior should now be evident. As was previously discussed, inductions and preachings that point out other people's feelings and the effects of a child's behavior on others appear to be effective at enhancing children's prosocial behavior. In addition, training procedures can be used to induce children to take the perspective of others and to help. An example of such a program is one designed by Norma Feshbach and her colleagues to reduce aggression and to promote prosocial responding. Children in their empathy training groups participated in activities designed to encourage children to think about other people's thoughts and feelings and to imagine how they would feel in a similar situation. Groups met three times a week for about 45 minutes for 10 weeks. Peers and teachers rated the children's prosocial behavior at the beginning of training, during training, and after training. Third- or fourth-graders who participated in these groups increased their prosocial responding relative to children who were in groups that discussed nonsocial problem-solving issues (such as a discovery science curriculum) or were not in either type of group.[47]

Based on research of this sort, numerous researchers and clinicians have argued that one of the most effective ways to enhance children's prosocial responding, reduce aggression, and promote the development of social skills is to use child-rearing techniques that help the child to understand the perspectives of other people and to empathize and sympathize with them.[48]

Michael Schulman and Eva Mekler, in their book *Bringing Up a Moral Child*, suggested that there are three foundation stones of moral development: (1) internalizing parental standards of right and wrong, (2) developing empathic reactions, and (3) acquiring personal standards. They also suggested a number of methods for encouraging children to develop empathic reactions:

1. Draw your child's attention to people's feelings. Ask him to imagine how he would feel in their place.
2. Let him know what the impact of his actions is on the feelings of others, including yourself.
3. Explain why people feel the way they do.
4. Make clear (or encourage him to discover) what actions he can take that would be more considerate.
5. Let him know that you expect him to be considerate, that it is important to you.
6. Let him know that you understand and care about *his* feelings and try to offer him a way to get at least some of what he wants—if not now, then in the future.

7. Don't expect him to read minds. Take the time to explain.
8. Help him understand other people's feelings by reminding him of similar experiences in his own life.
9. Help him resist the influence of people who discourage or ridicule his empathic feelings.
10. Give him approval when he is considerate. Show disappointment when he isn't.
11. Use self-control empathy training to teach him to imagine himself in someone else's place whenever he is inclined to hurt that person.
12. Share your own empathic feelings with him.
13. Point out examples of people who are empathic and those who are not, and communicate your admiration for kindhearted people.
14. Stress the good feelings that come from caring about other people.
15. Encourage him to consider a person's capacity for empathy when selecting friends.[49]

Shulman and Mekler's excellent suggestions reflect the research findings on the development of prosocial behavior and demonstrate how parents and other socializers can use the child's capacity for empathy to foster prosocial development.

How does one implement Schulman's and Mekler's suggestions? There are many opportunities in everyday life. Examples include news shows about people who have helped other people in emergency situations (for example, earthquakes) or in other distressing conditions, or about people who have protected and helped animals. Other examples include kind actions by peers or adults other than parents in the child's environment. Such situations provide opportunities to point out people who are empathic and to communicate that these people are admirable.

Disciplinary situations also provide excellent opportunities for encouraging perspective taking and empathy. Consider the following dialogue that could ensue when a preschool child has refused to share a swing with her sister, even after she has used it for a long time:

Parent:	I know that you are having a lot of fun on the swing, but your sister also likes to swing. She would like a turn.
Child:	But I don't want to get off.
Parent:	We know. But sometimes your sister lets you use the swing and her toys. And she has been waiting for a long time. So it's only fair to let her use the swing sometimes.
Child:	But I had it first.
Parent:	Yes, you did. But do you remember how you felt when your sister was watching TV first and wouldn't let you watch anything you wanted? You felt it wasn't fair, and she feels the same way now.

Such a conversation helps the child to understand *how* her sister feels, and *why*. Thus, the child is better able to feel what her sister is feeling and to take that into account.

These are just a few concrete examples of ways in which adults can foster children's perspective taking, empathy, and sympathy. Such techniques enhance the development of prosocial behaviors based on caring rather than on the desire for rewards or approval or the desire to avoid punishment.

THE INFLUENCE OF SIBLINGS

Parents are not the only family members who influence children's prosocial tendencies. In the United States, approximately 80 percent of children have at least one brother and sister, and by kindergarten they spend much more time with their siblings than with their parents.[50] Furthermore, sibling relationships have a different character from parent-child relationships; for example, siblings are more equal in status and therefore have many opportunities both to help one another and to be the recipient of assistance, comfort, or generosity. To quote Michael Lamb, "Siblings set and maintain standards, provide models to emulate and advice to consider, enact complementary roles in relation to one another through which both develop and practice social-interactional skills, and serve as confidant and sources of nonjudgmental social support in times of emotional stress."[51]

Sibling relationships are characterized both by negative behaviors such as aggressive, competition, and rivalry and by cooperative, prosocial interactions. Siblings frequently engage in cooperative task and help and share with one another.[52] Consider the following example of an 18-month-old:

> Sibling is crying bitterly, lying on M's [mother's] knee, face down. M attempts to comfort. C [child] watches soberly.
> M to C: What's wrong with Kelly?
> (C, with concerned expression, bends down, turns his head to look face to face at sib, strokes her hair.)[53]

Children as young as 14 months have been observed to show concern for their older siblings and to try to comfort them.[54] However, young children's helping or comforting of siblings may not always be appropriate to the needs of the sibling:

> Several incidents suggest that during the second year children begin to recognize that the distress of others can be relieved by the provision of comfort, but that what constitutes comfort for the other is not necessarily

identical to that which would constitute comfort for the child himself. There appears to be an awareness as early as 14 to 15 months that some of the acts within the child's power can provide some comfort for others, but the child may well overgeneralize the types of occasion or person for whom the action can be expected to provide comfort.[55]

In addition, young children sometimes turn to older siblings for comfort. Consider the report of one mother in a study of siblings: "Graham goes to him [Ian] for love and comfort. Saying 'ah' and screwing up his face as if to say 'Isn't he sweet!' Ian often comforts him, and he's very concerned when he's upset."[56]

Because of the amount of time siblings spend together, they appear to have a very good understanding of each other's feelings and frequently experience empathy for one another.[57] In the following real life example of empathy, 4-year-old Loren was at the doctor's with her 1-year-old sister, Katie. "Katie had an ear infection. The doctor looked in Katie's ear. Loren, who was watching, started to wail as if in great pain herself." Loren also would attempt to protect Katie from harm: "Katie accidentally banged into the edge of the table. Loren, who had observed this incident, got upset at the table. She hit the table and yelled at it, 'Don't hurt my baby!' "

Given the difference in the ability levels of older and younger children, it is not surprising that older siblings tend to help and comfort younger siblings more than the reverse.[58] Moreover, prosocial behavior between sibs seems to be more common in widely spaces than in closely spaced dyads and is slightly more common among same-sex siblings.[59] Siblings may get along better if they are not very close in age and are the same sex. In addition, girls are more prosocial than boys in their dealings with siblings; in many situations girls show higher levels of interest and involvement in caretaking and other activities with younger children than do boys.[60]

Younger children seem to imitate the prosocial behavior of their older brothers and sisters. For example, in one study 18-month-olds and an older sibling (an average of 26 months older) were observed in their homes. Toddlers whose older sibling was relatively prosocial tended to be more cooperative themselves. In addition, when the children were observed 6 months later, the more prosocial the toddler was, the more likely the older sibling was to interact cooperatively and to give the younger child something he or she would be interested in.[61] Thus, siblings seemed to influence each other's prosocial and cooperative tendencies. However, cooperation and prosocial behavior between siblings does not prevent conflict and aggression between them; in this same study, children who were particularly likely to attempt to share, help or comfort, and cooperate frequently got into conflicts with each other. This is not surprising, given the strong ambivalence that siblings often feel toward each other.

Sibling interactions are, of course, embedded in the interactions of the larger family unit. Thus, it is not surprising that parental attitudes and behaviors influence children's positive behaviors toward each other. One researcher investigated mothers and their elementary school daughters.[62] It found that mothers who were sensitive in their parenting behavior and did not ignore their children tended to have daughters who were relatively positive and prosocial in their interactions with one another, and who engaged in relatively few negative behaviors such as name calling and upsetting one another. Furthermore, preferential treatment by the

mother of one daughter over another was associated
with more negative interactions among sisters: "Thus, a
child's behavior related both to the way she was treated
by her mother and to the way her sister was treated. If
there was a discrepancy in treatment, she showed more
negative behavior toward her sister even when her own
needs were well met."[63]

In another study of mothers and their children, if a
mother discussed the newborn's feelings and needs
with an older sibling, the older child was more likely to
be affectionate and interested in the baby, to offer help,
and to cuddle the baby. This affection and interest in the
baby persisted over time. In comparison with older siblings who did not display interest in their newborn siblings, older siblings who were involved with newborns
in the first weeks of life were more likely 3 years later to
share toys or candy with them and to comfort them
when the latter were distressed. Further, when the
younger siblings of the friendly, interested children
were 14 months old, they were more likely than younger
sibs in other families to direct positive social behaviors
toward their older siblings.[64]

Maternal childrearing practices also appear to affect
whether or not older siblings are helpful, supportive,
and cooperative with their younger siblings. In a study
of school-age children (7 to 9 years) and their 4-to-6-
year-old siblings, older children's helping of the sibling
while playing in the home was associated with mothers'
reports of encouraging curiosity and openness and of
valuing having a separate life from their children. Mothers of prosocial children also were relatively consistent
in their discipline and tended not to use anxiety as a
form of punishment. In addition, mothers' use of non-
punitive disciplinary techniques and their enjoyment of
the maternal role were associated with more prosocial

behavior (for example, affection, praising, or engaging in cooperative joint play) and less negative behavior (for example, hitting, fighting, teasing, insulting, and negative facial expressions while interacting with the younger sibling). There were fewer correlations between mothers' reported childrearing practices and the behavior of the younger siblings. Nonetheless, mothers who tried to induce guilt in their children during disciplinary encounters had children who were not very cooperative and warm with their older siblings, and maternal inconsistency in discipline was related to low levels of younger siblings' helping and teaching their older siblings.[65]

Children's prosocial behavior, then, is influenced by the quality of their relationships and interactions with their siblings, and these in turn are affected by their relationships with their mothers. Children undoubtedly imitate one another and their parents; moreover, children's feelings of security and worth in the home seem to affect how they behave toward other people, as well as toward other family members.[66] Children who feel good about themselves and their relationships and are the recipients of prosocial behavior in the family are likely to develop helpful, caring attitudes and behaviors.

In summary, much socialization of prosocial behavior seems to occur in the family context. Parents of prosocial children tend to use inductive discipline, provide opportunities for their children to engage in prosocial actions, model and value prosocial behaviors, and encourage perspective taking, empathy, and sympathy. This is particularly true for children who have warm, secure relationships with their caretakers. In addition, the quality of children's relationships with siblings seems to influence children's prosocial tendencies, at least in social interactions with one another.

Socialization of prosocial tendencies within the home can have an enduring and profound effect on offspring's prosocial tendencies, as is illustrated by studies of real-life adult altruists such as the rescuers in Nazi-dominated Europe. Nonetheless, children's tendencies to help, share, comfort, and sympathize also are affected by influences outside the family. We now turn to these extrafamilial influences.

8 / Socialization outside the Home: School, Peers, and the Media

As children grow, they are increasingly exposed to the influence of people outside the home, including teachers, friends and other peers, neighbors, and people at religious institutions. In addition, children in industrialized societies are exposed indirectly to a number of people from around the world and to the ideas of other individuals through the media: telelvision, radio, movies, magazines, and newspapers. Therefore, the number of people who can potentially influence the development of children's prosocial tendencies increases as they develop, and these other influences may have a significant effect on the socialization of children's positive (and negative) behaviors.

We know much more about the influence of parents on children's prosocial development than about the effects of most socializers outside the home. Because of the ongoing debate about the effects of television on children, there has been a considerable amount of research on the effects of television viewing on children's behavior—mostly on aggression—although there is some research on the effects of prosocial television shows. In contrast, we have relatively little information about the influence of peers, teachers, and other people in the community on children's prosocial behavior.

Nonetheless, it seems obvious that teachers and peers must influence children's prosocial development. Once children enter school, they spend a large amount of time with teachers and friends. Furthermore, the importance of peer relationships to children increases with age, as does the amount of interaction with peers.[1] By adolescence, most children have very close relationships with at least one peer and spend much time with peers.[2]

In addition, children spend a shocking amount of time in front of the television. The average child in the United States spends more time watching television than in any other activity except sleep. Consequently, it is imperative that we understand how television is influencing our children's behavior and values.

TEACHERS AND SCHOOLS

Considering the amount of time children spend in school, we know relatively little about the effects of teachers or school structure and curriculum on children's prosocial development. However, we do know that they are important and can play a substantial role in shaping positive behavior.

Teachers are significant adults in children's lives and, consequently, serve as disciplinarians and as a source of values. They give instructions about helping and sharing and can encourage (or discourage) such activities. Moreover, like parents, they can serve as supportive, nurturant models or as cold, uncaring models.

Most of what has been found in the research about the influence of parents probably also pertains to some degree to teachers. Indeed, in much of the laboratory research on socialization practices, the "socializer" was a stranger, one who would be expected to have much less influence on children than would their teachers.

Thus, we can generalize from the laboratory research involving unknown adult socializers, as well as from the few studies involving teachers.

Teachers clearly serve as models of prosocial behavior; moreover, they are more frequently imitated by children if they are nurturant. In one study, nurturant adults who took part in preschool classes and who modeled prosocial behaviors had a relatively enduring influence on children's own prosocial behavior. In contrast, children did not model the prosocial behavior of cold, aloof adults in their classroom. Moreover, the adults' modeling of prosocial behavior was effective in increasing children's actual helping behavior only when the adults themselves engaged in real prosocial behaviors, and not when they enacted helping situations using only miniature toys (as in a play).[3] Thus, as in the home, teachers who were warm and modeled prosocial behaviors fostered children's helping and caring behavior.

In addition, teachers' verbalizations can enhance children's sharing behavior, depending on their content. In studies involving third- and fourth-graders, school principals who used empathy-inducing preachings in which they referred to the emotional state of poor children were successful in inducing children to share with poor children (through UNICEF). However, children exposed to principals who merely stated norms related to helping such as "Sharing is the right thing to do" were no more helpful than children who were not exposed to any preaching from the principals.[4] Thus, the notion that a good way to enhance children's prosocial behavior is to get them to take the perspective of others and to sympathize with them seems to hold in the school context.

In recent years there has been considerable debate in local communities and in the media about who is responsible for children's moral education—parents, teachers, or both. However, although many American educators have claimed that moral education is an important objective of the schools, moral education in the schools usually has been minimal. In most cases, the role of teachers in teaching morality has been limited and informal; teachers influence children by means of their modeling, preachings regarding good and bad behavior, and their rewards or punishments for behaviors such as sharing, cooperation, lying, stealing, and aggression. Most public schools and school districts have had neither the resources nor the inclination to explicitly try to teach children moral values and to encourage them to think about moral issues.

In fact, moral education has been considered much more important in some other countries than in the United States. For example, in some communist countries in which collective ownership has been part of the political doctrine, children have been explicitly taught to share, help, and cooperate from an early age. In China, teachers repeatedly tell students stories about altruistic heroes and encourage them to imitate these heroes. In addition, children are praised by teachers in front of the other children if they act in a helpful manner (for example, assist another child who has fallen).[5] Similarly, as was mentioned in Chapter 6, in the Soviet Union in the 1960s moral education was an explicit, stated goal of the schools. For example, 7- to 11-year-old students were expected to learn honesty, truthfulness, kindness, a sense of good and bad behavior, and friendship with classmates. Educational objectives for 16- to 18-year-olds included collectivism, conscience, and "socialist humanism." There values were strongly emphasized in classrooms and taught with a variety of methods. From the limited reports available, the children in Soviet schools seem to have developed cooperative and proso-cial behaviors and to have engaged in relatively little antisocial behavior.[6]

In the last couple of decades, some American educators have become concerned about the rates of aggression, delinquency, and other problems in our schools and have become interested in the possibility of moral education programs. A number of programs have been tried on a limited basis in some schools, often with some success. In most of these programs, the goal has been to stimulate higher-level moral reasoning (see Chapter 3); in only a relatively small number has the enhancement of children's sharing, helping, and concern for others been an explicit goal.

One program that was designed to enhance empathy and prosocial behavior and reduce aggression was discussed briefly in the last chapter. In this program, third- and fourth-graders were involved in several classroom activities designed to increase children's empathy; they learned how to recognize others' feelings, to understand their perspectives, to communicate effectively, and to imagine themselves in another's situation.[7] For example, in one set of classroom activities the objective was "to enhance role-playing skills. Specifically, to role play different characters and to develop alternative solutions to conflicts depicted in the dilemmas."[8] In this activity, some of the conflict dilemmas were:

A brother and sister want to watch two different television shows. They have an argument over which show they should watch. What can they do?

Wayne lets Sarah borrow his favorite toy. Sarah accidentally loses the toy, and Wayne is angry. They are arguing about what they should do about the lost toy. What can they do?[9]

The children formed a circle about 6 feet across and then read stories of this type one at a time. The children were told that the stories had no end, and that their job was to try to think of some ways to end them. Children also were told that they would act out the ideas suggested by the students, and that there were "lots of ways to finish each story." The instructions to the teacher were:

> It is important to stress generating alternative solutions. After a brief discussion, ask for volunteers to act out one of the solutions mentioned previously. The names and/or sexes of the characters in the vignettes can be changed to meet the needs of the children in the particular group. After the children have acted out one solution to the situation, it is a good idea to ask them to change roles and act out the story again.[10]

The goal of another activity was to learn that different emotions can be conveyed through varying tones of voice. In this activity, teachers and students discussed how the same sentence could mean different things, depending on the speaker's tone of voice. In addition, the teacher encouraged discussion of the types of circumstances that might cause sentences to be said in different ways, or the various roles that might cause people to use different tones of voice. For example, a communication to be discussed might be the sentence "Go to bed," said by a tired, frustrated mother, by a parent telling a sick child what to do, by a new babysitter begging a little child to go to bed, or by an angry older brother to a younger sibling.[11]

Such activities used in the classroom over an extended period of time (for example, 10 weeks) have proved to have positive effects on children's prosocial behavior, self-concepts, and social understanding. In addition, empathy training has been found to reduce aggressive behavior in children who were initially average or high in aggression.[12]

Educational programs also have been designed to increase cooperation in school settings, particularly cooperative learning. These cooperative learning programs differ somewhat in the degree to which their goals are primarily academic (that is, to increase learning) or are also social (that is, to enhance cooperation and prosocial development, or perhaps positive interactions between children from different ethnic and racial groups).[13]

In one type of cooperative learning procedure, called Small Group Teaching, children in a classroom work together in small groups on projects. For example, one program in Israel divided children in lower-socioeconomic class schools into as many as eight small groups per classroom: "Thus the classroom operates as a *peer society* organized into subunits each concentrated on some aspect of a broad learning task. These subunits provide its members with mutual help and support, collaboration on task-related activities, exchange of ideas and other resources, and mutual acceptance." To facilitate the effective functioning of these small groups, teachers were expected to

> assist pupils in acquiring sets of social skills, including: active listening to peers, utilizing others' ideas, sharing one's own thoughts and resources with others, respecting the speaking privileges of others, allowing the spontaneous emergence of informal leadership behaviors in a group, counteracting tendencies for power relations and concentration of dominance, and accepting responsibility for performing one's part in a division-of-labor structure . . . When these conditions prevail, they foster the emergence of role taking, empathy, friendship and close personal relations, and acceptance of others without regard to stereotyped attributions.[14]

Those in the small groups cooperative learning program gained both academically and socially in relation to children in traditional schools. They performed better on tests of higher-level thinking skills and creativity. They also reported a more positive social classroom climate, were more aware of prosocial values and goals, and were more helpful and cooperative, and less competitive and tense, when involved in tasks with other children (not necessarily those children in their own cooperative learning group).

A cooperative learning procedure that has been quite popular in the United States is the jigsaw technique. Children in a classroom are divided into groups of approximately six, and each child in a group is assigned a segment of a lesson, for example, a geography lesson on Mexico. Each child gathers and learns part of the necessary information, and then the children work together to complete the project. Thus, like parts of a jigsaw puzzle, they must come together and cooperate to complete their task successfully.[15] In a study in which sixth-graders met in their jigsaw groups for 45 minutes per day, three times a week for 6 weeks, children in the groups were more helpful, considerate, and cooperative than children who did not participate in jigsaw groups. In addition, they developed more positive attitudes toward school, their classmates, and themselves.[16]

School-based programs have also been developed to encourage kindness toward animals. The National Association for the Advancement of Humane Education, under the aegis of the Society for the Prevention of Cruelty to Animals, has developed a curriculum designed to "(1) assist children in developing compassion, a sense of justice, and a respect for all living creatures; (2) provide the knowledge and understanding necessary for children to behave according to these principles; and (3) foster a sense of responsibility on the part of children to affirm and act upon their personal beliefs."[17] The curriculum guides use a variety of teaching techniques, including perspective-taking activities, expression of feelings, discussion of values, storytelling, decision making, and creative writing.

According to an initial study, use of the curriculum can encourage humane attitudes toward animals. In this study, teachers of children in kindergarten to sixth grade used the curriculum with their students for an average of only 10 hours over a school year. Kindergarteners and first-graders who were exposed to the curriculum for only about 10 hours exhibited more humane attitudes toward animals than did children who were not exposed to the curriculum. Similar results were obtained for older children, but they were weaker (and not statistically significant). In a second study, a school-based humane education program was used for about 40 hours of classroom time in first-, second-, fourth-, and fifth-grade classes. On a self-report scale of empathy administered afterward, children who took part in the program scored higher than peers who did not. In addition, among first- and fourth-graders there was some evidence of an increase in humane attitudes toward animals. The findings demonstrate that children can be trained to extend their caring and concern to animals as well as to people, although it is likely that the effects of the program would be stronger if more class time were devoted to the curriculum.[18]

One of the larger school-based programs designed to increase children's prosocial behavior and cooperation is being conducted in the San Francisco Bay area. The project, called the Child Development Project, began in 1982 in three suburban elementary schools. Its goal is to "encourage the development of 'prosocial' characteristics in children, generally defined as attitudes, motives, and behaviors that reflect consideration of others' needs and feelings, concern for others' welfare, and a willingness to 'balance' one's own legitimate needs and desires with those of others in situations where they conflict."[19]

The children in this study have been followed since they were in kindergarten. These children have been exposed to an integrated set of classroom and school activities and procedures, as well as home activities. The five components of the program are: cooperative activities, activities promoting social understanding, highlighting prosocial values, helping activities, and developmental discipline. Cooperative learning activities are used in the classroom; interpersonal sensitivity and understanding are enhanced in the classroom through discussions of events that occur spontaneously in class (for example, conflicts among students, the presence of visitors from other cultures) and more formal activities designed to encourage perspective taking; and teachers model and endorse prosocial values and expose children to literature, films, and books that provide clear examples of prosocial models. Children are also encouraged to engage in helpful behaviors such as performing classroom chores, helping other students, and participating in tutoring and community and school service activities. Finally, teachers are encouraged to use developmental discipline:

> This is a *child-centered* approach to classroom management that works toward the development of self-control and personal commitment to rules and values through an emphasis on student understanding of the general principles behind rules, student autonomy, student input to and participation in rule-setting and decision-making, and the use of discipline practices centered around induction . . . mutual problem-solving (rather

than externally imposed rewards and punishments), and the use of minimal pressure necessary for obtaining compliance.[20]

In brief, the discipline used by teachers is the type that has been found to foster prosocial behavior in research on the socialization of helping, caring, and sharing (see Chapter 7).

As part of the project, teachers have received extensive training in how to implement the program's activities and in the use of child-centered discipline. Parents have been kept up to date with the project's activities through meetings and a newsletter.

The effects of the program have been assessed by means of observations of children in classes, on the playground, and participating in small group tasks. In addition, children have been interviewed and administered a variety of questionnaires, and teachers have evaluated the students' behaviors.

The results of the first 5 years of the program have been very encouraging. In comparison with children in schools without the program, students involved in the project have exhibited more supportive and friendly behavior and more spontaneous helpful, cooperative, and concerned behaviors. In interviews, they have exhibited greater perspective taking and consideration of others' needs and have been more likely to consider the consequences of their actions and to anticipate obstacles to resolving social conflicts. Program children chose strategies to deal with social conflicts that involved less aggression, more cooperation and prosocial behavior, and more planning. For example, they preferred strategies such as discussing a problem, explaining their position to the other person, and solutions involving sharing and compromise. In addition, they were more concerned than nonprogram children with the democratic value that all members of a group have a right to express their views and to be involved in group activities.

Clearly, school-based prosocial education programs such as the Child Development Project can have a significant effect on the development of prosocial and cooperative tendencies. Schools and teachers *can* instill prosocial values and behaviors in children on a school-wide basis, if the school's staff and parents are sufficiently motivated to do so. Many of the procedures used in prosocial training projects are easily integrated into the normal school routine and schedule and are not costly. Moreover, prosocial training programs need not impede academic progress; children in the child development project did not differ from other children in their schools on tests of academic achievement. Given the potential benefits of these training programs, teachers and school administrators should be encouraged to learn about and implement programs that foster prosocial development.

PEERS

A commonsense and prevalent belief is that children are influenced by their peers. Parents try to discourage their children from associating with the "wrong" kind of friends and encourage friendships with peers who exhibit desirable behaviors and attitudes. Obviously, parents and other socializers believe that children imitate and acquire the behaviors, attitudes, and values of their peers.

There is good reason for parents to be concerned about their children's peer relationships. Children, and particularly adolescents, invest a lot of time and emotional involvement in their friendships.[21] For example, in one study a substantial majority of adolescents answered "true" to the following statements:

"I have at least one close friend who means a lot to me" (94%).

"Once I become friends with someone, we stay friends a long time" (92%).

"My close friend understands me better than my parents do" (70%).

"I feel right now in my life I learn more from my close friend than I do from my parents" (68%).

"I'm more 'myself' with my close friend than with my parents" (68%).[22]

Children's friendships become more intense and intimate with age and are an important source of companionship and learning during childhood.[23]

Given the centrality of peers in children's lives, it is not surprising that peers *do* serve as socializers for one another. For example, by preschool age, children provide attention and approval to peers engaged in play with gender-typed toys (for example, dolls for girls or trucks for boys) and often ignore or desert peers who engage in opposite-sex activities.[24] Peers also help to shape one another's aggressive tendencies with their reactions to aggression,[25] and they serve as models of aggression, compliance with adults' prohibitions, and sociability.[26] In fact, peer models even influence food preferences.[27]

Not surprisingly, peers also serve as models of helpfulness, caring, and generosity. Children who view other children sharing, expressing sympathy, or helping someone are more likely to do so themselves.[28] Unfortunately, peers' selfish behaviors also are imitated, especially if the peer is not punished for his or her selfishness.[29]

Children also shape one another's prosocial and cooperative behaviors with their reactions to one another.

Preschool children are more likely to cooperate when their peers attend to their cooperative behaviors, and they inhibit their inappropriate behaviors (such as outbursts of aggression) if peers ignore them.[30] In fact, the influence of peers as socializers may be strong because children frequently respond to one another's prosocial behaviors. In one study in which 4- and 5-year-olds were observed for 9 weeks in their preschool classes, children responded positively to peers' unrequested (spontaneous) sharing and helping behaviors 30 percent of the time, and reacted positively (smiling, thanking the child, initiating social interaction or continuing to play with the other child) to 48 percent of the prosocial behaviors that they themselves requested of the peer.[31]

Peers may influence each other's prosocial development in yet other ways. In one study, withdrawn preschool children who were paired for a series of ten play sessions with another child became more sociable; in particular, they gave more positive reinforcement (defined as including help, guidance, praise, affection, reassurance, protection, gift giving, smiling, and cooperative play) to peers in their classroom after participating in the play sessions. The reasons for the effects are not fully understood, but it appeared that the play sessions provided opportunities for the socially withdrawn children to learn and practice positive social skills.[32]

Because the nature of relationships between children and adults and those between children differs dramatically, children may learn different things about sharing, helping, and caring from peers and from adults. In adult-child relationships, the adult is clearly the more powerful person—the one who can enforce his or her wishes if he or she wants to. Therefore, the child frequently must comply with the wishes of the adult. In contrast, peers are by definition more nearly equal in power and status, and neither is likely to always be the more dominant. Thus, peer relationships are more likely to involve cooperation between equals, sharing of ideas and input, and reciprocity.[33]

This difference in the two kinds of relationships appears to be reflected in children's conceptions of prosocial interactions with adults and peers. In one study, children aged 6 to 14 were asked to generate stories of adult-child or child-child interactions in which one person did something kind or unkind to the other, or to make judgments about the kindness of actors in stories. Young children (age 6 to 8) tended to define kindness toward adults as being obedient and as being good and polite, whereas unkindness was the reverse. The older children defined kindness toward adults not only as obedience and "being good," but also as doing one's chores and, occasionally, as showing concern for an adult in need. Typical responses about kindness toward adults were as follows:

"Love them and be nice."
"Putting the dishes away after dinner."
"Tell them you like them."
"Doing extra chores without being asked."
"By doing what they say."
"Obeying him."
"Do what they tell me and not talk back."
"Doing an errand to a sick grown-up."[34]

In contrast, children viewed peer-directed acts of kindness as involving giving and sharing, playing together, giving physical assistance, and occasionally (for older children) understanding or teaching.

"Give him some candy or ice cream . . . Because that was their friend."
"Give them things."

"Sharing . . . Because they like it."
"Play; do something with them."
"Ask them to do stuff with you."
"Like a new girl . . . other people poke fun. You make friends with her."
"One fell down. The other one could help him up."[35]

Thus children, particularly younger children, described acts of kindness toward adults as being characterized by obedience and compliance, whereas kindness toward peers involved more egalitarian and prosocial elements.[36]

This difference in children's perceptions of prosocial interactions with adults and peers is reflected in the reasons children give for helping and sharing with adults and peers in real life. When preschoolers were asked why they helped either adults (teachers or teachers' aides) or peers when requested to do so (by the other person) in their classroom, the answers they gave depended somewhat on who was the object of their generosity or helpfulness. Although children frequently referred to the other person's need or desire as a reason for helping or sharing, they did so more when discussing prosocial acts directed to other children. For example, children were likely to say they shared with a peer because "she wanted some clay" or helped because "he couldn't reach the crayons."[37]

In addition, children referred to their liking of the other person more often when discussing peer-directed prosocial behaviors than they did when discussing those directed toward adults. They gave reasons such as "I helped because he's my friend" or "Because I like him." In contrast, the children more often referred to punishments or to authority when discussing compliance with adults' requests. Examples of their reasons for helping included "She told me to" or "Because she's the teacher so I have to."[38]

Such findings suggest that children may learn somewhat different things about prosocial behavior from their interactions with peers and adults. Because they feel more nearly equal in interactions with peers, children may view their peer-directed prosocial behaviors as more voluntary than their adult-directed acts of kindness. In contrast, children (especially young children) may help or share with adults primarily because they feel they should or must. If this is true, children may be more likely to develop an altruistic self-perception in interactions with peers than in interactions with adults. Because the development of an altruistic self-image may lead children to be more prosocial in their future behavior (see Chapter 7), self-perceptions that emerge from interactions with peers could have important consequences for their prosocial development.

TELEVISION

The typical American child spends more time in front of the television than with parents, teachers, peers, or anyone else. By the time a child is 18 years old, he or she has spent over 15,000 hours watching television. Children begin watching television on a regular basis 3 or 4 years before entering first grade, and most children view television on a daily basis. It has been estimated that by the time children are 5, they have spent more time watching television than undergraduate liberal arts students spend in classrooms over 4 years. Inevitably, children will be influenced by the content of television programming because television characters model behaviors, verbalize values and attitudes, and communicate norms and standards. Consequently, the media must be considered important and pervasive socializers of our children. Moreover, given the status of many media stars for many youngsters, they are likely to be powerful models—ones that children desire to emulate.[39]

In recent decades there has been much debate about the consequences of television viewing, particularly the effects of exposing children to graphic violence. Consider the following case studies citing instances in which people imitated examples of aggression depicted on television:

> One is the film *Fuzz*, shown on television in Boston . . . starred Burt Reynolds as a city detective trying to catch a gang of youths who had been pouring gasoline over old men, described as "winos," and setting them afire. Their motive was described as "to get kicks." Two days after the film was shown, a young woman whose automobile had run out of gasoline was returning from a filling station with a can of gasoline when she was confronted by six youths. After dousing her with gasoline from the can, one of the youths set her afire. The young woman died some four hours later. In Miami, some three weeks later, a wino was sleeping on a bench when four youths poured gasoline over him and set him afire. He died as a result of his burns. The youths, when arrested, admitted to having seen the film, although they denied that was the reason for the attack. These two attacks were of a type previously unknown in the United States.[40]

Many other similar instances of imitation have been documented. A 17-year-old Kojak fan raped a 7-year-old the night after seeing a Kojak episode about a child molester. In Canada there was a television show about a real student who, in 1966, climbed to the top of the observation tower of the University of Texas campus in Austin and, with a high-powered rifle, killed 14 people and wounded 31 others. About 2 weeks after the show was aired in Toronto, a psychiatric patient bought a rifle and fired on pedestrians from the top of a 24-story building in Toronto. He killed 5 people, then committed suicide. The institution in which he stayed had aired that television show.[41]

These are obviously extreme examples. However, it is estimated that between the ages of 5 and 15, the average television viewer sees the violent destruction of more than 13,400 characters, as well as hundreds of rapes, assaults, and other crimes.[42] It is hard to imagine that exposure to so much violence has no impact on the developing child.

In fact, evidence from many studies, using a variety of methods, indicates that television violence has a causal effect on aggressive behavior in children and adolescents.[43] For example, in one 22-year-long study that followed subjects from childhood, 8-year-olds who were heavy viewers of violent television shows were more aggressive than their peers who watched less violent television, and were more aggressive and had been convicted of more serious crimes 22 years later.[44] Laboratory studies in which children were exposed to violent television for a relatively brief period also indicate that children are sometimes more violent after exposure to television violence.[45]

Clearly, television can be a negative influence on children; but can it also be a positive influence? If children model and learn from violent television shows and movies, they would be expected to learn positive behaviors and values from shows depicting helpfulness, generosity, cooperation, self-sacrifice, and the like. Recent studies suggest that the media can be used to foster positive development, although the effects of viewing prosocial television programming appear to be somewhat weaker than the effects of viewing violent programming.

In one such study, fourth-, seventh-, and tenth-graders viewed one of three television shows: (1) an edited action drama from commercial television in which the adult characters responded constructively to an interpersonal conflict, (2) a version of the same show edited so that the adults responded aggressively to the conflict, and (3) a wildlife documentary that depicted neither antisocial nor prosocial behavior. Then the students were given an opportunity to either help or hurt a fictitious peer who was completing a task elsewhere; the students could press a "help" button that shut off a distracting noise for the peer or a "hurt" button that increased the noise. Children exposed to the television in which the adults behaved in a constructive manner helped more than children in either of the other two groups.[46]

In another study, children who had viewed an episode of the television show "Lassie" in which the dog Lassie was saved from harm by her master were more likely to help puppies in distress than were other children, even if helping interfered with the children's earning points toward a prize.[47] Similarly, exposure to prosocial television shows such as "Mister Rogers' Neighborhood" has been found to increase lower socioeconomic preschoolers' prosocial behavior (for example, cooperation, nurturance, and sympathy).[48]

However, it appears that the effects of exposure to prosocial programming are relatively modest, and that they may be weaker than the effects of exposure to training procedures aimed at increasing children's perspective-taking skills.[49] Thus, it has been suggested that it might be fruitful to use prosocial television as one component in larger training programs aimed at fostering prosocial development.[50] In addition, socializers can capitalize on prosocial television programming by using it as a vehicle for discussing prosocial heroes and the thoughts and feelings of others.

*   *   *

Socialization may begin at home, but children are soon exposed to other people who influence the development of prosocial and cooperative tendencies. In addition, the outside world, including violence and other forms of antisocial behavior, is brought into the home through television, the newspapers, videotapes, and other forms of mass communication. Consequently, it is essential to consider the roles of teachers, schools, peers, and the mass media in children's moral development. Caregivers can promote positive behaviors and values in their children not only through their own interactions with the children, but also by influencing school curricula, monitoring children's use of media, and taking steps to influence public policy related to schools and television.

9/ The Effect of Circumstances

Children are not equally helpful, generous, or caring in all situations. This is not surprising; a major finding in psychological research is that people's behavior is influenced by aspects of their immediate situation as well by their individual personal characteristics. Although there is some tendency toward consistency of behavior across different situations, behavior undeniably changes as the context does.[1]

For example, what a person chooses to eat for lunch on a given day may be influenced not only by his or her personal food preferences, but also by (among other things) the cost of the various restaurants in the vicinity, how much time the person has for lunch, whether or not the individual is alone, the food preferences of the individual's lunch companions, and the time he or she ate breakfast (and how big it was). Yet a long-term study of the person's behavior would probably yield systematic patterns, influenced by both the individual's characteristics and the situation. For example, on days when other people are available for lunch, our person may tend to go to one or two restaurants where it is easy to talk and the food is acceptable to most people, whereas when there is little time and no one else is

available for lunch, he or she may tend to buy a sand-
wich from a nearby fast-food establishment or skip
lunch altogether.

Children's and adults' helping, sharing, and comforting behaviors are also affected by their situation. Some
fairly dramatic examples can be found in the Oliners'
book *The Altruistic Personality*, which studied the motives of people who either helped or did not help Jews
to escape Nazi persecution. The Oliners persuasively
argued that rescuers and nonrescuers differed more in
character than in opportunities to assist Jews; that is,
they differed more in values and degree of caring than
in economic resources, knowledge of the persecution,
or the potential risk to themselves of helping. Nonetheless, there were some differences in the situations in
which rescuers and nonrescuers tended to find themselves. Rescuers, more than nonrescuers, tended to be
embedded in a social network that was supportive of
rescuing activities:

> More important than formally organized resistance net-
> works were the informal ones rescuers created out of
> their own contacts with families, friends, and others
> personally known to them . . . What apparently distin-
> guished rescuers from nonrescuers was not access to or
> potential for organizing such informal networks, but
> rather the sentiments and behaviors of their networks—
> the types of people who comprised their most intimate
> contacts. More rescuers had reason to believe that their
> contacts would support them. More rescuers belonged
> to formal networks that shared their concerns about
> Jews. And more rescuers could assume that their fami-
> lies would help them if called on, because of their own
> activities.[2]

In fact 60 percent of rescuers had at least one other
family member who was involved in rescue or resis-

tance activities, in contrast to 20 percent for people who reported no rescuing activities. In some cases, many members of a single church or village were involved in efforts to help the Jews.[3]

People who were embedded in social networks favorable to rescuing activities not only were more likely to find more support for rescue efforts; they also were more likely than other people to be asked by friends, relatives, or acquaintances to become involved in rescue activities. Sixty-seven percent of rescuers did not become involved in helping Jews until someone, often an intermediary acting on a victim's behalf, asked if they were willing to assist. Fewer nonrescuers had been asked to assist. Of course, whether or not someone was asked to help depended in part on the person's reputation and attitudes; people unlikely to be receptive to helping were unlikely to be asked to assist. Nonetheless, many rescuers might not have become involved if they had not been asked to do so in a single specific situation. And some rescuers might not have assisted had they not felt that their friends and families would support their activities.

This is a dramatic example of how aspects of a situation can influence whether or not a person decides to behave prosocially. In everyday life, too, there are numerous factors, many of them trivial, that appear to influence whether or not, and when, people choose to share, assist, or offer sympathy to others.

MOOD STATES

Temporary mood states—for example, whether we feel good, sad, anxious, or neutral—influence many aspects of people's behavior, including whether individuals help and share with others.

FEELING GOOD

Think about times when you are happy. Often people in a good mood feel positive toward other people and the world in general, and optimistic. Consequently, it is not surprising that both children and adults are more likely to help or share with others when they feel this way.[4]

A feeling of happiness can be created by as fleeting an event as hearing a joke, winning a small prize, finding a dime, or recalling a good memory. For example, in one study, 7- and 8-year-olds were asked to reminisce about either happy or sad events, whereas other children simply counted numbers. Then all children were given the opportunity to share anonymously some of the money they earned for participating. The children who had reminisced about happy events shared more than did the children who had either thought about sad events or merely counted.

The effects of temporary mood probably last only as long as the mood itself. For example, in one study, adults tended to be willing to help a stranger immediately after they received a small gift, but not 20 minutes later.[5]

But in some contexts, positive moods do not promote prosocial behavior. For example, happiness may not enhance prosocial behavior in some competitive contexts. Children who have been successful in competitive games are less likely to share with the losers than are children who did not win.[6]

It is not entirely clear why happy people are more prosocial. In addition to feeling more optimistic and positive about other people when they are happy, they may feel less vulnerable and less in need of protecting resources.[7] People in positive moods may also be better able to retrieve positive memories about past helping acts and, therefore, be more willing to assist.[8] Whatever the reasons, when children feel good, generosity and helping are more forthcoming.

FEELING SAD OR BAD

The effects of feeling bad are more complex than the effect of a positive mood. Children who experience temporary sadness generally are less likely to assist others often than children in neutral or happy moods. Negative moods can stem from thinking about sad events or negative events such as losing a game.[9]

However, sometimes children in negative moods are relatively helpful and generous. For instance, when children have failed at a task and then are given an opportunity to share in the presence of the adult who witnessed their failure, they are relatively generous. Perhaps they feel they can compensate for their loss of status in the adult's eyes by behaving in a socially desirable, laudable manner.[10] In addition, as was discussed in Chapter 4, children who feel negative because of empathic sadness or sympathy for distressed or needy people are relatively likely to help or share.

In general, however, temporary negative moods appear to increase adults' prosocial behavior but to decrease children's (with the exception of sympathy).[11] One explanation for this pattern is that adults assist others when they are in a negative mood to make themselves feel better. The argument is that during socialization, older children learn that the performance of prosocial actions can alleviate negative moods because prosocial acts—which often are praised and rewarded—gradually become associated with positive feelings and become reinforcing in themselves.[12]

Support for this explanation is mixed.[13] Other explanations for the findings have been suggested. For example, some investigators have proposed that negative mood increases prosocial behavior when the mood is caused by attention to the negative states of other people, whereas children's prosocial behavior is unaffected or decreased if they are in a negative mood, because they are attending to issues related to themselves.[14] Presumably, a focus on other people's negative states facilitates sympathetic responding, whereas a focus on oneself results in depression, personal distress, or self-concern.

COSTS AND BENEFITS OF A PROSOCIAL ACT

Children, like adults, are more likely to perform prosocial acts that are low in cost to themselves and have obvious benefits for the potential recipient.[15] For example, children share disliked toys more than favored toys[16] and are more likely to give up recess time to assist an injured peer if they do not like recess.[17] They also share or help more if the beneficiary is poor or is obviously doing poorly on a task.[18] Thus, the type of assistance required and its potential impact are important determinants of when children assist others.

CHARACTERISTICS OF THE RECIPIENT OF AID

Children, like adults, help some people more than they do others.[19] For example, as was just discussed, they are more likely to share with needy or poor people than with non-needy people,[20] as well as with friendless children.[21] In addition, children's prosocial behavior is affected by a variety of characteristics of a potential recipient, including the latter's demographic characteristics and relationship to the child.

As one might expect, children often assist or share

with people they know and like more than other people. For example, 1- to 2-year-olds prefer to offer or show an object to parents than to siblings or strangers,[22] and both children and adults assist people who are similar to themselves (for example, people from the same neighborhood or ethnic background or people who have similar interests and beliefs) more than they assist those who are dissimilar.[23] Young children are particularly likely to say that they would help primarily family members and friends, and would not assist disliked others or those of a different background.[24] However, the tendency to favor people whom one knows and likes, or who are similar, may decrease somewhat with age, perhaps because, with increasing age, children learn to perspective take and sympathize with a wider range of people and to view moral principles and values as being applicable to most or all people.[25]

Alternatively, adults simply may be more covert and subtle than children in their discrimination against potential recipients who are different from themselves. Adults are particularly likely to fail to assist someone of another race when they can attribute their failure to help to factors other than race.[26] In contrast, in the few relevant studies involving children, it is not clear that white children assist or share with other Caucasians more than with people of other races—even though they say they have a preference for assisting those from a similar ethnic group.[27] Perhaps young children sometimes have not yet fully adopted the larger society's discriminatory attitudes, with the result that they do not view peers from a different racial group as very different from themselves (unless they are labeled as being from a different group).

Clearly, children empathize more readily with friends and similar people (for example, same-sex children or children from a similar racial background) than with other people.[28] Thus, in most situations one would expect children to help and share with friends more than other people. However, children sometimes assist nonfriends more than friends. They probably are more likely to favor nonfriends when they feel secure about the friendship,[29] or when they are involved in a competition in which the competitors' performances will be compared.[30] Children, like adults, also may feel less constrained to reciprocate friends' prosocial actions immediately or in equal measure.[31]

Because children seem to prefer directing behaviors toward known and familiar people, it is not surprising that young children behave more prosocially toward same-sex than toward other-sex children.[32] However, this tendency to favor same-sex peers decreases with age,[33] and adolescent and adult males help females more than males (females in these age groups assist males and females approximately equally).[34]

Children also are more likely to behavior prosocially toward popular than unpopular children,[35] persons considered to be likable,[36] and other prosocial children.[37] In addition, children tend to help or share with people who have helped or shared with them in the past or who might reciprocate in the future.[38] Although as they grow older children tend to consider such reciprocity-based prosocial behavior as less kind and altruistic,[39] the tendency to assist people who are likely to reciprocate may increase with age in the elementary school years.[40]

Finally, although children tend to favor assisting needy persons, they also tend to discriminate in regard to whom they consider to be worthy of aid. Children attend to the factors that are responsible for the other person's need, and they are relatively unlikely to assist people whose need is perceived to be within their own control (for example, is the result of laziness or carelessness).[41] Thus, children share more money with other children who have never had money than with children who have carelessly lost their own money.[42] It is likely that children base their prosocial responding primarily on the potential recipient's deservedness when there are no other more salient factors (for example, similarly to the self) to influence their decision whether or not to help.[43]

Children's prosocial behavior, then, is influenced by a variety of characteristics of the potential recipient in a particular context. Some people—for example, prosocial, popular, and needy children—are more likely to elicit prosocial behavior from other children, and children are particularly likely to assist people similar to themselves or people whom they know and like.

FACTORS AFFECTING HELPING IN EMERGENCIES

As was discussed in Chapter 1, much of the initial research on prosocial behavior concerned situational factors that affect when adults help in emergencies. Investigators found that adults are more likely to help someone in distress—for example, someone who has fainted or has had a seizure—if they are alone rather than in a group.[44] Adults who are alone may fail to help because they are afraid of being evaluated negatively by bystanders if they have misinterpreted the situation and offer help unnecessarily. In addition, adults frequently may not interpret an emergency as such if other bystanders have not responded, and they also may feel that others in a group may be more competent at helping or should take responsibility for assisting.

In contrast to the many studies on adults' helping in emergencies, there is little research concerning factors that affect children's emergency interventions. It is not even clear whether children, like adults, are less likely to assist in emergencies if other people are present.[45] In some contexts children, particularly older children, may be inhibited by concern about a peer's evaluation,[46] although children sometimes help more when they are with peers.[47] Whether or not children help when peers are present may depend on who and where the peer is (for example, in the same room or out of sight) and on the child's age. Moreover, children seem to be more likely to assist in emergencies and in everyday situations when they have been implicitly or explicitly assigned responsibility.[48] Thus, it is likely that children's helping in emergencies—like many other prosocial behaviors—is influenced by a variety of situational factors, as well as by personal characteristics such as the child's social assertiveness.[49]

10/ Conclusion

After more than two decades of empirical study of prosocial development, what do we know about the development and maintenance of prosocial responding?

As in the behavioral and social sciences in general (and even the physical sciences), knowledge is seldom absolute. What we know changes with new information and the development of new conceptual frameworks for interpreting data. Nonetheless, it is possible to draw a number of tentative conclusions about prosocial development.

THE CURRENT STATE OF KNOWLEDGE

First, prosocial behavior takes many forms and emerges early in life—in most cases by the second year. This is much earlier than was predicted by most theorists a few decades ago. Young children are capable of understanding others' feelings, at least to some degree, and of responding with sympathy and prosocial action. Like adults, young children do not always respond prosocially when confronted with a needy or distressed person, but the capacity for prosocial responding—and perhaps even altruistic responding—is evident early in life.

Children's thinking about other people's feelings and perspectives, and their own moral reasoning, change somewhat with age; moreover, these changes appear to be reflected, to some degree, in children's prosocial responding. Children become more overtly and self-consciously other-oriented and less self-oriented with age. In addition, they are increasingly able to understand the perspectives of others and abstract moral principles; these developmental changes are reflected in children's moral reasoning and in the motives behind their prosocial actions. Thus, an important age-related change is an increase in children's capacity to enact altruistic behaviors based on internalized moral principles and their understanding of the perspectives of people who are unknown or the perspective of the larger group or society.

As is obvious from casual observation, not all people are equally prosocial or altruistic. Prosocial children tend to be sympathetic and capable of relatively mature levels of moral reasoning and perspective taking. In addition, children who are spontaneously helpful and generous are likely to be sociable, assertive, and socially competent. Of course, children who perform prosocial actions primarily to secure positive outcomes for themselves (for example, rewards and social approval) probably differ from children who tend to perform altruistic prosocial behaviors aimed at alleviating another's need, and it is the latter group of children that are particularly likely to be sympathetic, high moral reasoners, and capable of taking others' perspectives.

Although it is clear that children differ in their altruistic tendencies, it is difficult to determine the causes of these individual differences. Biological factors may play a role. For example, relatively extroverted children and those who are better able to regulate their physiological and emotional responding (characteristics that appear to have some biological bases) may be particularly likely to experience sympathy rather than personal distress and, consequently, may be more altruistic. However, at this time we know relatively little about the biological bases of individual differences in prosocial responding. In contrast, there is substantial evidence indicating that both the larger society and individuals in the child's social world influence children's prosocial and altruistic tendencies. Children learn values and specific behaviors from family members, peers, and teachers, as well as from the media and other societal institutions. Children learn from observing others' behaviors and from the values, attitudes, and cognitions communicated to them. In addition, whether or not children tend to focus on other people's needs and sympathize with them seems to depend, in part, on how the child is disciplined and nurtured, and on the values and attitudes toward other people communicated to the child in the disciplinary context. In general, cultures and families are likely to produce prosocial children when cooperation, helpfulness, generosity, and harmony are valued and modeled, children are loved and treated with respect, and the similarity of diverse groups of people is emphasized.

In the final analysis, however, whether or not children behave prosocially depends on the interaction between the particular circumstances of the situation and the child's individual characteristics—characteristics that result from both biological factors and socialization experiences. Specific situations foster certain types of behaviors, but more so for some children than for others. Moreover, on the basis of their individual characteristics and experiences, different children may interpret the same situation quite differently. Thus, when considering individual differences in children's prosocial responding, it is important to consider the context in which the prosocial behavior is observed or assessed.

The multiple factors that influence children's prosocial responding, and the interaction of these factors, are depicted in simplified schematic form in Figure 1.[1] Unfortunately, researchers have seldom been able to study the role of more than one or two of the influences on prosocial development simultaneously, so our understanding of the precise nature of the interactions among personal characteristics, and between situational variables and personal characteristics, is limited. Nonetheless, it is clear that our conceptualizations of prosocial development cannot be limited to the consideration of biological, socialization, personal, or situational variables in isolation.

NEW DIRECTIONS

Although there is still much to learn about prosocial behavior and its development, some gaps in our knowledge are more obvious and pressing than others. In addition, some questions that have not yet been adequately addressed are of greater practical importance than others.

A very important and perhaps surprising gap in our understanding concerns programs for enhancing altruistic tendencies. Several programs have been successful in fostering generosity, helpfulness, and considerate behavior (see Chapter 8), but they are few in number, and generally their effects are not well understood. In most of the intervention programs instituted in real-life settings, in order to ensure a positive result investigators have tended to use every procedure likely to foster prosocial development simultaneously, rather than test-

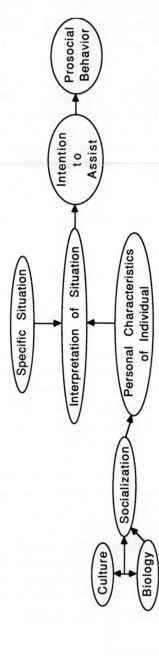

Figure 1. Factors influencing prosocial behavior. *Source:* Adapted from Nancy Eisenberg, *Altruistic Emotion, Cognition, and Behavior* (Hillsdale, N.J.: Lawrence Erlbaum Associates, 1986).

ing the effectiveness of individual components of programs. This strategy is an appropriate one when the goal is merely to ascertain whether it is possible to devise a successful intervention program. However, now that it is clear that school-based intervention programs can enhance prosocial responding and cooperation, they should be streamlined to include only elements that are effective. Because time and money for such programs are limited, it is important that researchers now try to identify which elements (for example, the use of developmental discipline, procedures for cooperative learning, or activities designed to promote social understanding) are effective and which are not so that programs can be implemented as economically as possible.

Another area in which more information is needed is the role of extrafamilial influences such as peers, clubs, neighbors, churches, and schools in prosocial development. We know relatively little about how these people and institutions affect children's prosocial values and behaviors, and we know even less about the ways in which these influences interact with familial influences in fostering or undermining prosocial development. For example, the degree to which extrafamilial influences can counter the influences of parents and siblings is unknown. Nor do we know if teachers, peers, and institutions such as the schools and churches can adequately promote children's prosocial development if prosocial behavior is not fostered in the family environment. These are issues of practical and conceptual importance.

In addition, although we know quite a bit about the development of prosocial behavior, we know somewhat less about the factors that specifically promote *altruistic* prosocial behaviors. Children can perform prosocial actions for many reasons, and the factors associated with

the promotion of altruistic rather than egoistically motivated prosocial behavior have not yet been adequately
isolated. One way to study the development of true
altruism is to examine the lives of people whose altruistic motivation has been relatively clear—that is, to
study exemplars of moral behavior such as Mahatma
Gandhi. Another more feasible method is to conduct
in-depth research on people alive today who have been
involved in humanitarian endeavors. An excellent example of such research is the Oliners' study (see Chapter 8) of people who rescued jews in Nazi Europe.[2] With
intensive interviews and testing, it is possible to examine the motives, background, and experiences of those
persons who have exhibited altruistic motives and behaviors. In such studies we may also begin to isolate the
multiple interrelated factors—environmental and
personal—that appear to have influenced altruistic people's reasoning and behavior.

The last few years have been times of startling change,
some good and some bad. In 1989, countries such as
Poland and Czechoslovakia without bloodshed gained
the right of self-determination. However, the newfound
freedom in eastern Europe has been combined with increases in ethnic violence and antisemitism. In South
Africa, Nelson Mandela, who fought apartheid from
prison for 27 years, has finally been released, in part as
a result of worldwide pressure and concern for human
rights. However, violence among different groups in
South Africa persists. As the world grows ever smaller
in terms of the ease of interaction among peoples, and
as the population of the earth continues to grow, the
need for cooperation among countries, concern for others, and mutual aid and support among different groups
of people increases. If people do not learn to live to-

gether in harmony, the consequences promise to be disastrous for us all.

The study of prosocial behavior is very important if we hope to reduce and perhaps someday even eliminate the injustice, inhumanity, and violence that have been constant features of human history. An understanding of prosocial behavior and altruism could be used to implement changes in schools, in the media, and even in government policies that affect the resources and values of families—changes that could help to humanize our attitudes, values, and behaviors. Although such interventions would be costly, controversial, and difficult to implement, the alternative—continuing the pattern of inequality, dehumanization, and aggression—is costlier still.

Notes

1 / THE STUDY OF PROSOCIAL BEHAVIOR

1. D. Hume, *Enquiries concerning the Human Understanding and concerning the Principles of Morals.* 2d ed. (1777; reprint, Oxford: Clarendon Press, 1966).

2. T. W. Adorno, E. Frenkel-Brunswick, D. J. Levinson, and R. N. Sanford, *The Authoritarian Personality* (New York: Harper, 1950); S. Milgram, *Obedience to Authority: An Experimental View* (New York: Harper & Row, 1974).

3. B. Latane and J. Darley, *The Unresponsive Bystander: Why Doesn't He Help?* (New York: Appleton, 1970).

4. N. Eisenberg, "The Development of Reasoning about Prosocial Behavior," in *The Development of Prosocial Behavior* (New York: Academic Press, 1962); idem, *Altruistic Emotion, Cognition, and Behavior* (Hillsdale, N.J.: Lawrence Erlbaum Associates, 1986); M. L. Hoffman, "Developmental Syntheses of Affect and Cognition and Its Implications for Altruistic Motivation," *Developmental Psychology* 11 (1975):607–622; N. Eisenberg and P. H. Mussen, *The Roots of Prosocial Behavior in Children* (Cambridge: Cambridge University Press, 1989); J. F. Rushton, *Altruism, Socialization, and Society* (Englewood Cliffs, N.J.: Prentice-Hall, 1980); E. Staub, *Positive Social Behavior and Morality, vol. 1: Social and Personal Influences* (New York: Academic Press, 1978); idem, *Positive Social Behavior and Morality,* vol. 2: *Socialization and Development,* (New York: Academic Press, 1979).

5. J. F. Dovidio, "Helping Behavior and Altruism: An Em-

pirical and Conceptual Overview," in *Advances in Experimental Social Psychology*, ed. L. Berkowitz, vol. 17 (New York: Academic Press, 1984); D. L. Krebs and D. T. Miller, "Altruism and Aggression," in *Handbook of Social Psychology*, ed. G. Lindzey and E. Aronson, 3d ed., vol. 2 (New York: Random House, 1985).

6. D. Bar-Tal, "American Study of Helping Behavior. What? Why? and Where?" in *Development and Maintenance of Prosocial Behavior: International Perspectives on Positive Behavior*, ed. E. Staub, D. Bar-Tal, J. Karylowski, and J. Reykowski (New York: Plenum Press, 1984).

2 / BENEVOLENT BABIES AND CARING CHILDREN

1. J. Piaget and B. Inhelder, *The Child's Conception of Space* (London: Routledge and Kegan Paul, 1956).

2. One of the leading contributors to research concerning the early development of prosocial behavior is Judith Dunn. See J. Dunn, *The Beginnings of Social Understanding* (Cambridge, Mass.: Harvard University Press, 1988), especially her chapter "Benevolent Babies."

3. G. B. Martin and R. D. Clark III, "Distress Crying in Neonates: Species and Peer Specifically," *Developmental Psychology* 18 (1987):3–9; M. L. Hoffman, "Sex Differences in Empathy and Related Behaviors," *Psychological Bulletin* 84 (1977):712–722.

4. D. F. Hay, A. Nash, and J. Pedersen, "Responses of Six-Month-Olds to the Distress of Their Peers," *Child Development* 52 (1981):1071–75.

5. M. Radke-Yarrow and C. Zahn-Waxler, "Roots, Motives, and Patterns in Children's Prosocial Behavior," in *Development and Maintenance of Prosocial Behavior: International Perspectives on Positive Behavior*, ed. E. Staub, D. Bar-Tal, J. Karylowski, and J. Reykowski (New York: Plenum Press, 1984), p. 89.

6. M. L. Hoffman, "Development of Prosocial Motivation: Empathy and Guilt," in *The Development of Prosocial Behavior*, ed. N. Eisenberg (New York: Academic Press, 1982).

7. C. Zahn-Waxler and M. Radke-Yarrow, "The Development of Altruism: Alternative Research Strategies," in Eisenberg, *The Development of Prosocial Behavior*.

8. M. L. Hoffman, "Development of Prosocial Motivation: Empathy and Guilt," in Eisenberg, *The Development of Prosocial Behavior*. (Cambridge: Cambridge University Press, 1982), p. 287.

9. C. Zahn-Waxler, M. Radke-Yarrow, and R. A. King, "Child Rearing and Children's Prosocial Initiations toward Victims of Distress," *Child Development* 50 (1979):319–330.

10. Radke-Yarrow and Zahn-Waxler, "Roots, Motives, and Patterns," p. 89.

11. Dunn, *The Beginnings of Social Understanding*, p. 90.

12. J. Dunn and C. Kendrick, "Siblings and Their Mothers: Developing Relationships within the Family," in *Sibling Relationships*, ed. M. C. Lamb and B. Sutton-Smith (Hillsdale, N.J.: Lawrence Erlbaum Associates, 1982), p. 115.

13. Radke-Yarrow and Zahn-Waxler, "Roots, Motives, and Patterns."

14. Hoffman, "Development of Prosocial Motivation," pp. 287–288.

15. Zahn-Waxler and Radke-Yarrow, "The Development of Altruism."

16. Dunn, *The Beginnings of Social Understanding*.

17. C. Howes and J. Farver, "Toddlers' Responses to the Distress of Their Peers," *Journal of Applied Developmental Psychology* 8 (1987):441–452.

18. D. F. Hay, "Cooperative interactions and Sharing between Very Young Children and Their Parents," *Developmental Psychology* 15 (1979):647–653; H. L. Rheingold, D. F. Hay, and M. J. West, "Sharing in the Second Year of Life," *Child Development* 47 (1976):1148–58.

19. T. Kitwood, *Concern for Others: A New Psychology of Conscience and Morality* (London: Routledge, 1990), p. 103.

20. Hay, "Cooperative Interactions and Sharing."

21. H. L. Rheingold, "Little Children's Participation in the Work of Adults: A Nascent Prosocial Behavior," *Child Development* 53 (1982):114–125.

22. Dunn, *The Beginnings of Social Understanding*.

23. Hoffman, "Development of Prosocial Motivation," p. 288.

24. N. Eisenberg-Berg and M. Hand, "The Relationship of Preschoolers' Reasoning about Prosocial Moral Conflicts to Prosocial Behavior," *Child Development* 50 (1979):356–363; R. J. Iannotti, "Naturalistic and Structured Assessments of Prosocial Behavior in Preschool Children: The Influence of Empathy and Perspective Taking," *Developmental Psychology* 21 (1970):46–55; F. F. Strayer, S. Wareing, and J. P. Rushton, "Social Constraints on Naturally Occurring Preschool Altruism," *Ethology and Sociobiology* 1 (1979):3–11.

25. N. Eisenberg, J. F. Pasternack, E. Cameron, and K. Tryon, "The Relation of Quantity and Mode of Prosocial to Moral Cognitions and Social Style," *Child Development* 55 (1984):1479–85; Eisenberg-Berg and Hand, "Preschoolers' Reasoning about Prosocial Moral Conflicts"; Strayer, Wareing, and Rushton, "Social Constraints on Preschool Altruism."

26. Hoffman, "Development of Prosocial Motivation"; Eisenberg-Berg and Hand, "Preschoolers' Reasoning about Prosocial Moral Conflicts"; M.R. Yarrow and C. Z. Waxler, "Dimensions and Correlates of Prosocial Behavior in Young Children," *Child Development* 47 (1976):118–125.

27. M. Radke-Yarrow, C. Zahn-Waxler, and M. Chapman, "Prosocial Dispositions and Behavior," in *Manual of Child Psychology*, ed. E. M. Hetherington, vol. 4: *Socialization, Personality, and Social Development*, ed. P. Mussen (New York: John Wiley & Sons, 1983).

28. N. Eisenberg and J. Pasternack, "Inequalities in Children's Prosocial Behavior: Whom Do Children Assist?" in *The Child's Construction of Social Inequalilty*, ed. R. Leahy (New York: Academic Press, 1983); N. Eisenberg, E. Cameron, K. Tryon, and R. Dodez, "Socialization of Prosocial Behavior in the Preschool Classroom," *Developmental Psychology* 17 (1981):773–782; Strayer, Wareing, and Rushton, "Social Constraints on Preschool Altruism."

29. T. J. Berndt and T. B. Perry, "Children's Perceptions of

Friendships as Supportive Relationships," *Development Psychology* 22 (1986):640–648.

30. P. W. Berman, "Children Caring for Babies: Age and Sex Differences in Response to Infant Signals and to the Social Context," in *Contemporary Topics in Developmental Psychology*, ed. N. Eisenberg (New York: John Wiley & Sons, 1987); S. S. Feldman, S. C. Nash, and C. Cutrona, "The Influence of Age and Sex on Responsiveness to Babies," *Developmental Psychology* 13 (1977):675–676.

31. B. R. Burleson, "The Development of Comforting Strategies in Childhood and Adolescence," *Child Development* 53 (1982):1578–88.

32. M. L. Hoffman, "Interaction of Affect and Cognition in Empathy," in *Emotions, Cognitions, and Behavior*, ed. C. E. Izard, J. Kagan, and R. B. Zajonc (Cambridge: Cambridge University Press, 1984).

33. Radke-Yarrow, Zahn-Waxler, and Chapman, "Prosocial Dispositions and Behavior."

34. B. K. Bryant and S. B. Crockenberg, "Correlates and Dimensions of Prosocial Behavior: A Study of Female Siblings with Their Mothers," *Child Development* 51 (1980):529–544; G.W. Ladd, G. Lange, and A. Stremmel, "Personal and Situational Influences on Children's Helping Behavior: Factors That Mediate Compliant Helping," *Child Development* 54 (1983):488–501; Radke-Yarrow, Zahn-Waxler, and Chapman, "Prosocial Dispositions and Behavior."

35. L. Peterson, "Role of Donor Competence, Donor Age, and Peer Presence on Helping in an Emergency," *Developmental Psychology* 19 (1983):873–880.

36. E. Midlarsky and M. E. Hannah, "Competence, Reticence, and Helping by Children and Adolescents," *Developmental Psychology* 21 (1985):534–541; E. Staub, "A Child in Distress: The Effects of Focusing Responsibility on Children on Their Attempts to Help," *Developmental Psychology* 2 (1970):152–153.

37. Ibid., L. Peterson, "Influence of Age, Task Competence, and Responsibility Focus on Children's Altruism," *Developmental Psychology* 19 (1983):141–148.

38. K. Barnett, G. Darcie, C. J. Holland, and A. Kobasigawa, "Children's Cognitions about Effective Helping," *Developmental Psychology* 18 (1982):267–277.

39. D. Bar-Tal and R. Nissim, "Helping Behavior and Moral Judgment among Adolescents," *British Journal of Development Psychology* 2 (1984):329–336.

3 / MOTIVES FOR PROSOCIAL ACTIONS

1. D. Bar-Tal, "Sequential Development of Helping Behavior: A Cognitive-Learning Approach," *Developmental Review* 2 (1982):101–124.

2. N. Eisenberg, "The Development of Reasoning about Prosocial Behavior," in *The Development of Prosocial Behavior*, ed. N. Eisenberg (New York: Academic Press, 1982); idem, *Altruistic Emotion, Cognition, and Behavior* (Hillsdale, N.J.: Lawrence Erlbaum Associates, 1986).

3. Eisenberg, *Altruistic Emotion, Cognition, and Behavior*.

4. N. Eisenberg-Berg, "Development of Children's Prosocial Moral Judgment," *Developmental Psychology* 15 (1979): 128–137.

5. N. Eisenberg, J. F. Pasternack, E. Cameron, and K. Tryon, "The Relation of Quantity and Mode of Prosocial to Moral Cognitions and Social Style," *Child Development* 55 (1984): 1479–85; N. Eisenberg and C. Neal, "Children's Moral Reasoning about Their Own Spontaneous Prosocial Behavior," *Developmental Psychology* 15 (1979):228–229.

6. N. Eisenberg, N. Lundy, R. Shell, and K. Roth, "Children's Justifications for Their Adult and Peer-Directed Complaint (Prosocial and Nonprosocial) Behaviors," *Developmental Psychology* 21 (1985):325–331.

7. J. Piaget, *The Moral Judgment of the Child* (1932; reprint, New York: Free Press, 1965); J. Youniss, *Parents and Peers in Social Development: A Sullivan-Piaget Perspective* (Chicago: University of Chicago Press, 1980).

8. Bar-Tal, "Sequential Development of Helping Behavior."

9. D. Bar-Tal, A. Raviv, and T. Leiser, "The Development

of Altruistic Behavior: Empirical Evidence," *Developmental Psychology* 16 (1980):516–524.

10. Ibid.; A Raviv, D. Bar-Tal, and T. Lewis-Levin, "Motivations for Donation Behavior by Boys of Three Different Ages," *Child Development* 51 (1980):610–613.

11. Bar-Tal, Raviv, and Leiser, "The Development of Altruistic Behavior."

12. D. Bar-Tal and R. Nissim, "Helping Behavior and Moral Judgment among Adolescents," *British Journal of Development Psychology* 2 (1984):329–336; J. Guttman, D. Bar-Tal, and T. Leiser, "The Effect of Various Reward Situations on Children's Helping Behavior" (manuscript, Tel Aviv University, 1979).

13. E. Midlarsky and M. E. Hannah, "Competence, Reticence, and Helping by Children and Adolescents," *Developmental Psychology* 21 (1985):534–541.

14. M. A. Barnett, S. Thompson, and J. Schroff, "Reasons for Not Helping," *Journal of Genetic Psychology* 148 (1987):489–498.

15. L. Kohlberg, "Moral Stage and Moralization: The Cognitive-Developmental Approach," in *Moral Development and Behavior: Theory Research and Social Issues*, ed. T. Lickona (New York: Holt, Rinehart and Winston, 1976); idem, *The Philosophy of Moral Development: Moral Stages and the Idea of Justice* (San Francisco: Harper & Row, 1981); idem, *Essays on Moral Development*, vol. 2: *The Psychology of Moral Development* (San Francisco: Harper & Row, 1984).

16. Eisenberg, "The Development of Reasoning about Prosocial Behavior"; idem, *Altruistic Emotion, Cognition, and Behavior*; N. Eisenberg, R. Shell, J. Pasternack, R. Lennon, R. Beller, and R. M. Mathy, "Prosocial Development in Middle Childhood: A Longitudinal Study," *Developmental Psychology* 23 (1987):712–718.

17. N. Eisenberg, K. Boehnke, P. Schuhler, and R. K. Silbereisen, The Development of Prosocial Behavior and Cognitions in German Children," *Journal of Cross-Cultural Psychology* 16 (1985):69–82; H. Munekata and K. Ninomiya, "Development of Prosocial Moral Judgments," *Japanese Journal of Educational Psychology* 33 (1985):157–164.

18. I. Fuchs, N. Eisenberg, R. Hertz-Lazarowitz, and R. Sharabany, "Kibbutz, Israeli City, and American Children's Moral Reasoning about Prosocial Moral Conflicts," *Merrill-Palmer Quarterly* 32 (1986):37–50; J. R. Snarey, "Cross-Cultural Universality of Socio-Moral Development: A Critical Review of Kohlbergian Research," *Psychological Bulletin* 97 (1985):202–232.

4 / CHARACTERISTICS OF PROSOCIAL CHILDREN

1. J. H. Block, "Conceptions of Sex Role: Some Cross-Cultural and Longitudinal Perspectives," *American Psychologist* 28 (1973):512–526; C. C. Shigetomi, D. P. Hartmann, and D. M. Gelfand, "Sex Differences in Children's Altruistic Behaviors and Reputations for Helpfulness," *Developmental Psychology* 17 (1981):434–437.

2. J. Dunn and P. Munn, "Siblings and the Development of Prosocial Behavior," *International Journal of Behavioral Development* 9 (1986):265–284; N. Eisenberg, S. A. Wolchik, L. Goldberg, and I. Engel, "Parental Values, Reinforcement, and Young Children's Prosocial Behavior," *Journal of Genetic Psychology* (in press).

3. N. Eisenberg and P. H. Mussen, *The Roots of Prosocial Behavior in Children* (Cambridge: Cambridge University Press, 1989); R. C. Savin-Williams, *Adolescence: An Ethological Perspective* (New York: Springer-Verlag, 1987).

4. D. Baumrind, "Current Patterns of Parental Authority," *Developmental Psychology Monographs* 4 (1971):1–103.

5. D. Baumrind, personal communicationa, cited in P. Mussen and N. Eisenberg-Berg, *Roots of Caring, Sharing, and Helping: The Development of Prosocial Behavior in Children* (San Francisco: Freeman, 1977).

6. J. P. Rushton and J. Wiener, "Altruism and Cognitive Development in Children," *British Journal of Social and Clinical Psychology* 14 (1975):341–349; E. Dlugokinski and I. J. Firestone, "Congruence among Four Methods of Measuring Other-Centeredness," *Child Development* 44 (1973):304–308; N. Eisenberg, R. Shell, J. Pasternack, R. Lennon, R. Beller,

and R. M. Mathy, "Prosocial Development in Middle Childhood: A Longitudinal Study," *Developmental Psychology* 23 (1987):712–719.

7. S. A. Small, R. S. Zeldin, and R. C. Savin-Williams, "In Search of Personality Traits: A Multimethod Analysis of Naturally Occurring Prosocial and Dominance Behavior," *Journal of Personality* 51 (1983):1–16; Savin-Williams, *Adolescence: An Ethological Perspective.*

8. M. Radke-Yarrow and C. Zahn-Waxler, "Roots, Motives, and Patterns in Children's Prosocial Behavior," in *Development and Maintenance of Prosocial Behavior: International Perspectives on Positive Behavior,* ed. E. Staub, D. Bar-Tal, J. Karylowski, and J. Reykowski (New York: Plenum Press, 1984), p. 92.

9. M. Radke-Yarrow, C. Zahn-Waxler, and M. Chapman, "Prosocial Dispositions and Behavior," in *Manual of Child Psychology,* ed. E. M. Hetherington, vol. 4: *Socialization, Personality, and Social Development,* ed. P. Mussen (New York: John Wiley & Sons, 1983); B. Underwood and B. S. Moore, "The Generality of Altruism in Children," in *The Development of Prosocial Behavior,* ed. N. Eisenberg (New York: Academic Press, 1982).

10. P. W. Berman, "Are Women More Responsive than Men to the Young? A Review of Developmental and Situational Variables," *Psychological Bulletin* 88 (1980):668–695; Shigetomi, Hartmann, and Gelfand, "Sex Differnces in Children's Altruistic Behaviors"; L. Zarabatany, D. P. Hartmann, D. M. Gelfand, and P. Vinciguerra, "Gender Differences in Altruistic Reputation: Are They Artifactual?" *Developmental Psychology* 21 (1985):97–101.

11. P. W. Berman, "Children Caring for Babies: Age and Sex Differences in Response to Infant Signals and to the Social Context," in *Contemporary Topics on Developmental Psychology,* ed. N. Eisenberg (New York: John Wiley & Sons, 1987); A. H. Eagly and M. Crowley, "Gender and Helping Behavior: A Meta-Analytic Review of the Social Psychological Literature," *Psychological Bulletin* 100 (1986):283–308.

12. B. I. Fagot, "The Influence of Sex of Child on Parental

Reactions to Toddler Children," *Child Development* 49 (1978):459–465; T. G. Power and R. D. Parke, "Patterns of Early Socialization: Mother- and Father-Infant Interaction in the Home," *International Journal of Behavioral Development* 9 (1986):331–341.

13. Eisenberg and Mussen, *The Roots of Prosocial Behavior in Children*.

14. L. Berkowitz, "Responsibility, Reciprocity, and Social Distance in Help Giving: An Experimental Investigation of English Social Class Difference," *Journal of Experimental Social Psychology* 4 (1968):46–63; L. Berkowitz and P. Friedman, "Same Social Class Differences in Helping Behavior," *Journal of Personality and Social Psychology* 5 (1967):217–225.

15. Eisenberg and Mussen, *The Roots of Prosocial Behavior in Children*.

16. A. Raviv, D. Bar-Tal, H. Ayalon, and A. Raviv, "Perception of Giving and Receiving Help by Group Members," *Representative Research in Social Psychology* 11 (1980):140–151; E. Staub, "A Child in Distress: The Influence of Age and Number of Witnesses on Children's Attempts to Help," *Journal of Personality and Social Psychology* 14 (1970):130–140.

17. B. B. Whiting and J. W. M. Whiting, *Children of Six Cultures: A Psycholocultural Analysis* (Cambridge, Mass.: Harvard University Press, 1975).

18. M. Summers, "Imitation, Dominance, Agonism, and Prosocial Behavior: A Meta-Analysis of Sibling Behavior" (Paper presented at the biennial meeting of the Society for Research in Child Development, Baltimore, April 1987).

19. S. A. Denham, "Social Cognition, Prosocial Behavior, and Emotion in Preschoolers: Contextual Validation," *Child Development* 57 (1986):194–201; N. Eisenberg, E. Cameron, K. Tryon, and R. Dodez, "Socialization of Prosocial Behavior in the Preschool Classroom," *Developmental Psychology* 17 (1981):773–782; R. Lennon and N. Eisenberg, "Gender and Age Differences in Empathy and Sympathy," in *Empathy and Its Development*, ed. N. Eisenberg and J. Strayer (Cambridge: Cambridge University Press, 1987); J. Strayer, "A Naturalistic Study of Empathic Behaviors and Their Relation to Affective

States and Perspective-Taking Skills in Preschool Children," *Child Development* 51 (1980):815–822.

20. C. A. C. Bergin, "Relations among Prosocial Behaviors in Toddlers" (Paper presented at the biennial meeting of the Society for Research in Child Development, Baltimore, April 1987); Eisenberg, Cameron, Tryon, and Dodez, "Socialization in the Preschool Classroom"; L. Stanhope, R. Q. Bell, and N. Y. Parker-Cohen, "Temperament and Helping Behavior in Preschool Children," *Developmental Psychology* 23 (1987):347–353.

21. W. Suda and G. Fouts, "Effects of Peer Presence on Helping in Introverted and Extroverted Children," *Child Development* 51 (1980):1272–75.

22. L. B. Murphy, *Social Behavior and Child Personality* (New York: Columbia University Press, 1937); M. R. Yarrow and C. Z. Waxler, "Dimensions and Correlates of Prosocial Behavior in Young Children," *Child Development* 47 (1976):118–125.

23. Eisenberg, Cameron, Tryon, and Dodez, "Socialization in the Preschool Classroom"; J. A. Larrieu, "Prosocial Values, Assertiveness, and Sex: Predictors of Children's Naturalistic Helping" (Paper presented at the biennial meeting of the Southwestern Society for Research in Human Development, Denver, March 1984).

24. Yarrow and Waxler, "Dimensions and Correlates of Prosocial Behavior"; D. E. Barrett, "Relations between Aggressive and Prosocial Behaviors in Children," *Journal of Genetic Psychology* 134 (1979):317–318.

25. Eisenberg, Cameron, Tryon, and Dodez, "Socialization in the Preschool Classroom"; N. Eisenberg, H. McCreath, and R. Ahn, "Vicarious Emotional Responsiveness and Prosocial Behavior: Their Interrelations in Young Children," *Personality and Social Psychology Bulletin* 14 (1988):298–311.

26. J. Block and J. H. Block, "Ego Development and the Provenance of Thought: A Longitudinal Study of Ego and Cognitive Development in Young Children," progress report for the National Institute of Mental Health (Grant No. MH16080) (January 1973); J. A. Larrieu, "Children's Commitment to Others, Social Efficacy, and Prosocial Behavior" (Pa-

per presented at the biennial meeting of the Southwestern Society for Research in Human Development, Denver, March 1984); J. Larrieu and P. Mussen, "Some Personality and Motivational Correlates of Children's Behavior," *Journal of Genetic Psychology* 147 (1986):529–542.

27. R. B. Hampson, "Adolescent Prosocial Behavior: Peer Group and Situational Factors Associated with Helping," *Journal of Personality and Social Psychology* 45 (1984):153–162; K. D. McGuire and J.R. Weisz, "Social Cognition and Behavior Correlates of Preadolescent Chumship," *Child Development* 53 (1982):1478–84; see Eisenberg and Mussen, *The Roots of Prosocial Behavior in Children*.

28. M. O'Connor, S. Dollinger, S. Kennedy, and P. Pelletier-Smetko, "Prosocial Behavior and Psychopathology in Emotionally Disturbed Boys," *American Journal of Orthopsychiatry* 49 (1979):301–310.

29. D. Hume, *Enquiries concerning the Human Understanding and concerning the Principles of Morals*, 2d ed. (1777; reprint, Oxford: Clarendon Press, 1966), pp. 219–220.

30. N. Eisenberg, *Altruistic Emotion, Cognition, and Behavior* (Hillsdale, N.J.: Lawrence Erlbaum Associates, 1986); M. L. Hoffman, "Interaction of Affect and Cognition in Empathy," in *Emotions, Cognition, and Behavior*, ed. C. E. Izard, J. Kagan, and R. B. Zajonc (Cambridge: Cambridge University Press, 1984); E. Staub, "Steps toward a Comprehensive Theory of Moral Conduct: Goal Orientation, Social Behavior, Kindness, and Cruelty," in *Morality, Moral Behavior, and Moral Development*, ed. W. M. Kurtines and J. L. Gewirtz (New York: John Wiley & Sons, 1984).

31. C. D. Batson, "How Social an Animal? The Human Capacity for Caring," *American Psychologist* 45 (1990):336–346.

32. M. L. Hoffman, "Development Synthesis of Affect and Cognition and Its Implications for Altruistic Motivation," *Developmental Psychology* 11 (1975):615.

33. S. P. Oliner and P. M. Oliner, *The Altruistic Personality: Rescuers of Jews in Nazi Europe* (New York: Free Press, 1988).

34. N. Eisenberg, R. A. Fabes, P. A. Miller, J. Fultz, R. Shell, R. M. Mathy, and R. Reno, "Relation of Sympathy and

Personal Distress to Prosocial Behavior: A Multimethod Study," *Journal of Personality and Social Psychology* 57 (1989):55–66; see C. D. Batson, "Prosocial Motivation: Is It Ever Truly Altruistic?" in *Advances in Experimental Social Psychology*, ed. L. Berkowitz, vol. 20 (New York: Academic Press, 1987); N. Eisenberg and P. A. Miller, "The Relation of Empathy to Prosocial and Related Behavior," *Psychological Bulletin* 101 (1987):91–119.

35. Eisenberg and Miller, "The Relation of Empathy to Prosocial and Related Behavior."

36. N. Eisenberg and R. Lennon, "Sex Differences in Empathy and Related Capacities," *Psychological Bulletin* 94 (1983):100–131; Eisenberg and Miller, "The Relation of Empathy to Prosocial and Related Behavior"; M. L. Hoffman, "The Measurement of Empathy," in *Measuring Emotions in Infants and Children*, ed. C. E. Izard (Cambridge: Cambridge University Press, 1982).

37. D.R. Weston and M. Main, "Infant Responses to the Crying of an Adult Actor in the Laboratory: Stability and Correlates of 'Concerned Attention' " (Paper presented at the Second International Conference on Infant Studies, New Haven, Conn., April 1980).

38. R. Lennon, N. Eisenberg, and J. Carroll, "The Relation between Empathy and Prosocial Behavior in the Preschool Years," *Journal of Applied Developmental Psychology* 7 (1986):219–224.

39. Eisenberg, McCreath, and Ahn, "Vicarious Emotional Responsiveness and Prosocial Behavior."

40. Eisenberg et al., "Sympathy and Personal Distress"; N. Eisenberg, R. A. Fabes, P. A. Miller, R. Shell, C. Shea, and T. May-Plumlee, "Preschoolers' Vicarious Emotional Responding and Their Situational and Dispositional Prosocial Behavior," *Merrill-Palmer Quarterly* 36 (1990):507–529.

41. D. L. Krebs and B. Sturrup, "Role-Taking Ability and Altruistic Behavior in Elementary School Children," *Journal of Moral Education* 11 (1982):94–100; P. Mussen, E. Rutherford, S. Harris, and C. Keasey, "Honesty and Altruism among Preadolescents," *Developmental Psychology* 3 (1970):169–194;

Rushton and Wiener, "Altruism and Cognitive Development in Children"; see Eisenberg and Mussen, *The Roots of Prosocial Behavior in Children.*

42. C. V. Shantz, "The Development of Social Cognition," in *Review of Child Development Research,* ed. E. M. Hetherington, vol. 5 (Chicago: University of Chicago Press, 1975).

43. Hoffman, "Developmental Syntheses of Affect and Cognition," p. 621.

44. B. Underwood and B. Moore, "Perspective-Taking and Altruism," *Psychological Bulletin* 91 (1982):143–173.

45. L. M. Hudson, E. A. Forman, and S. Brion-Meisels, "Role Taking as a Predictor of Prosocial Behavior in Cross-Age Tutors," *Child Development* 53 (1982):1320–29.

46. D. E. Barrett and M. R. Yarrow, "Prosocial Behavior, Social Inferential Ability, and Assertiveness in Young Children," *Child Development* 48 (1977):475–481; L. Peterson, "Influence of Age, Task Competence, and Responsibility Focus on Children's Altruism," *Developmental Psychology* 19 (1983):141–148; idem, "Role of Donor Competence, Donor Age, and Peer Presence on Helping in an Emergency," *Developmental Psychology* 19 (1983):873–880.

47. C. Tomlinson-Keasey and C. B. Keasey, "The Mediating Role of Cognitive Development in Moral Judgment," *Child Development* 45 (1974):291–298; L. J. Walker, "Cognitive and Perspective-Taking Prerequisites for Moral Development," *Child Development* 51 (1980):131–139; L. J. Walker and B. S. Richards, "Stimulating Transitions in Moral Reasoning as a Function of Cognitive Development, *Developmental Psychology* 15 (1979):95–103.

48. Eisenberg, *Altruistic Emotion, Cognition, and Behavior;* L. Kohlberg and D. Candee, "The Relationship of Moral Judgment to Moral Action," in Kurtines and Gewirtz, *Morality, Moral Behavior, and Moral Development;* Underwood and Moore, "Perspective-Taking and Altruism."

49. Eisenberg et al., "Prosocial Development in Middle Childhood"; N. Eisenberg and R. Shell, "Prosocial Moral Judgment and Behavior in Children: The Mediating Role of Cost," *Personality and Social Psychology Bulletin* 12 (1986):426–

433; N. Eisenberg-Berg and M. Hand, "The Relationship of Preschoolers' Reasoning about Prosocial Moral Conflicts to Prosocial Behavior," *Child Development* 50 (1979):356–363.

50. D. Bar-Tal, "Sequential Development of Helping Behavior: A Cognitive-Learning Approach," *Developmental Review* 2 (1982):101–124.

51. Eisenberg and Shell, "Prosocial Moral Judgment and Behavior in Children"; see Eisenberg, *Altruistic Emotion, Cognition, and Behavior.*

5 / THE BIOLOGICAL BASES OF ALTRUISM

1. E. O. Wilson, *Sociobiology: The New Synthesis* (Cambridge, Mass.: Harvard University Press, 1975).

2. Ibid., p. 121.

3. Ibid., pp. 121–122.

4. D. J. Hayes, R. R. Felton, and R. R. Cohen, "A Natural Occurrence of Foster Parenting by a Female Mountain Bluebird," *Auk*, 1985, pp. 191–193.

5. Wilson, *Sociobiology*, p. 128.

6. Ibid.; E. O. Wilson, *On Human Nature* (Cambridge, Mass.: Harvard University Press, 1978); W. D. Hamilton, "The Genetical Evolution of Social Behavior," *Journal of Theoretical Biology* 7 (1964):1–52; idem, "Selection of Selfish and Altruistic Behavior in Some Extreme Models," in *Man and Beast: Comparative Social Behavior*, ed. J. F. Eisenberg and W. S. Dillon (Washington, D.C.: Smithsonian Institution Press, 1972).

7. Wilson, *Sociobology*, pp. 3–4.

8. N. L. Segal, "Cooperation, Competition, and Altruism within Twin Sets: A Reappraisal," *Ethology and Sociobiology* 5 (1984):163–177.

9. D. Bar-Tal, Y. Bar-Zohar, M. S. Greenberg, and M. Hermon, "Reciprocity Behavior in the Relationship between Donor and Recipient and between Harm-Doer andVictim," *Sociometry* 40 (1977):293–298; S. M. Essock-Vitale and M. T. McGuire, "Women's Lives Viewed from an Evolutionary Perspective: II. Patterns of Helping," *Ethology and Sociobiology* 6 (1985):155–174.

10. M. R. Cunningham, "Levites and Brother's Keepers: A Sociobiological Perspective on Prosocial Behavior," *Humboldt Journal of Social Relations* 13 (1986):35–67.

11. J. P. Rushton, "Genetic Similarity, Human Altruism, and Group Selection," *Behavioral and Brain Sciences* 12 (1989):503–559; J. P. Rushton, R. J. H. Russell, and P. A. Wells, "Genetic Similarity Theory: Beyond Kin Selection," *Behavior Genetics* 14 (1984):179–193.

12. R. L. Trivers, "The Evolution of Reciprocal Altruism," *Quarterly Review of Biology* 46 (1971):35–57; idem, "The Evolution of Cooperation," in *The Nature of Prosocial Development*, ed. D. L. Bridgeman (New York: Academic Press, 1983).

13. Hayes, Felton, and Cohen, "Foster Parenting by a Female Mountain Bluebird."

14. J. Hill, "Human Altruism and Sociocultural Fitness," *Journal of Social and Biological Structures* 7 (1984):17–35; P. D. MacLean, "Evolutionary Brain Roots of Family, Play, and the Isolation Call" (Paper presented at the annual meeting of the American Psychiatric Association, Toronto, May 1982); C. J. Lumsden and E. O. Wilson, *Genes, Mind, and Culture: The Co-evolutionary Process* (Cambridge, Mass.: Harvard University Press, 1981).

15. J. P. Rushton, D. W. Fulker, M. C. Neal, D. K. B. Nias, and H. J. Eysenck, "Altruism and Aggression: The Heritability of Individual Differences," *Journal of Personality and Social Psychology* 50 (1986):1192–98.

16. K. A. Matthews, C. D. Batson, J. Horn, and R. H. Rosenman, "Principles in His Nature Which Interest Him in the Fortune of Others: The Heritability of Empathic Concern for Others," *Journal of Personality* 49 (1981):237–247.

17. R. Plomin, *Development, Genetics, and Psychology* (Hillsdale, N.J.: Erlbaum and Associates, 1986).

18. Lumsden and Wilson, *Genes, Mind, and Culture*.

6 / CULTURAL INFLUENCES

1. C. M. Turnbull, *The Mountain People* (New York: Simon and Schuster, 1972), p. 135.

2. Ibid., p. 234.

3. R. P. Rohner, *They Love Me, They Love Me Not* (New Haven: HRAF Press, 1975), p. 149.

4. Ibid.

5. Quoted in ibid., p. 152.

6. R. Benedict, *Patterns of Culture*, 6th ed. (Boston: Houghton Mifflin, 1934), p. 173.

7. Ibid., pp. 190–191.

8. Ibid., pp. 215, 216.

9. N. B. Graves and T. D. Graves, "The Cultural Context of Prosocial Development: An Ecological Model," in *The Nature of Prosocial Development*, ed. d. L.Bridgeman (New York: Academic Press, 1983); J. H. Honigman, *Personality in Culture* (New York: Harper & Row, 1967); M. Mead, *Sex and Temperament in Three Primitive Societies* (New York: Morrow, 1935); Rohner, *They Love Me, They Love Me Not*; A. Tietjen, "Prosocial Reasoning among Children and Adults in a Papua New Guinea Society," *Developmental Psychology* 22 (1986):861–868.

10. Graves and Graves, "The Cultural Context of Prosocial Development," pp. 247–248.

11. Ibid.

12. N. Eisenberg, A. Tietjen, R. K. Silbereisen, P. Schuhler, R. Hertz-Lazarowitz, I. Fuchs, and K. Boehnke, "Prosocial Moral Judgment: Cross-Cultural Research," in *Altruistic Emotion, Cognition, and Behavior*, ed. N. Eisenberg (Hillsdale, N.J.: Lawrence Erlbaum Associates 1986); Tetjen, "Prosocial Reasoning in a Papua New Guinea Society," p. 172.

13. Rohner, *They Love Me, They Love Me Not*, p. 135.

14. Honigman, *Personality in Culture*, p. 220.

15. W. Dennis, *The Hopi Child* (New York: John Wiley & Sons, 1965); Honigman, *Personality in Culture*.

16. M. E. Spiro, "Education in a Communal Village in Israel," in *Education and Culture*, ed. G. Spindler (New York: Holt, Rinehart, and Winston, 1963), p. 478.

17. A. Shapiro and M. C. Madsen, "Cooperative and Competitive Behavior of Kibbutz and Urban Children in Israel," *Child Development* 40 (1969):609–617.

18. C. C. Chao, G. P. Knight, and A. F. Dubro, "Informa-

tion Processing and Age-Differences in Social Decision Making," *Developmental Psychology* 22 (1986):500–508; Graves and Graves, "The Cultural Context of Prosocial Development"; S. Kagan and M. C. Madsen, "Experimental Analyses of Cooperation and Competition of Anglo-American and Mexican Children," *Developmental Psychology* 6 (1972):49–59.

19. See S. Kagan, "Social Motives and Behaviors of Mexican-American and Anglo-American Children," in *Chicano Psychology*, ed. J. L. Martinez (New York: Academic Press, 1977).

20. S. Kagan, G. P. Knight, and S. Martinez-Romero, "Culture and the Development of Conflict Resolution Style," *Journal of Cross-Cultural Psychology* 13 (1982):43–58; M. C. Madsen, "Cooperative and Competitive Motivation of Children in Three Mexican Sub-Cultures," *Psychological Reports* 20 (1967):1307–20; idem, "Developmental and Cross-Cultural Differences in the Cooperative and Competitive Behavior in Young Children," *Journal of Cross-Cultural Psychology* 2 (1971):365–371; M. C. Madsen and A. Shapiro, "Cooperative and Competitive Behavior of Urban Afro-American, Anglo-American, Mexican-American, and Mexican Village Children," *Developmental Psychology* 3 (1970):16–20.

21. A. Shapiro and J. Lomranz, "Cooperative and Competitive Behavior of Rural Arab Children in Israel," *Journal of Cross-Cultural Psychology* 3 (1972):353–359; Shapiro and Madsen, "Kibbutz and Urban Children in Israel"; idem, "Between- and Within-Group Cooperation and Competition among Kibbutz and Nonkibbutz Children," *Developmental Psychology* 10 (1974):140–145.

22. G. Marin, B. Mejia, and C. DeOberle, "Cooperation as a Function of Place of Residence in Columbian Children," *Journal of Social Psychology* 95 (1975):127–128; M. C. Madsen and S. Yi, "Cooperation and Competition of Urban and Rural Children in the Republic of Korea," *International Journal of Psychology* 10 (1975):269–274.

23. R. L. Munroe and R. H. Munroe, "Cooperation and Competition among East African and American Children," *Journal of Social Psychology* 101 (1977):145–146; E. A. Sommer-

lad and W. P. Bellingham, "Cooperation-Competition: A Comparison of Australian and European and Aboriginal School Children," *Journal of Cross-Cultural Psychology* 3 (1972):149–157; D. R. Thomas, "Cooperation and Competition among Polynesian and European Children," *Child Development* 46 (1975):948–953.

24. D. W. Bethleheim, "Cooperation, Competition, and Altruism among School Children in Zambia," *International Journal of Psychology* 8 (1973):125–135; M. Toda, H. Shinotsuka, C. G. McClintock, and F. J. Stech, "Development of Competitive Behavior as a Function of Culture, Age, and Social Comparison," *Journal of Personality and Social Psychology* 36 (1978):825–839.

25. Sommerlad and Bellingham, "Cooperation-Competition."

26. A. G. Miller, "Integration and Acculturation of Cooperative Behavior among Blackfoot Indian and Non-Indian Canadian Children," *Journal of Cross-Cultural Psychology* 4 (1973):374–380; A. G. Miller and R. Thomas, "Cooperation and Competition among Blackfoot Indian and Urban Canadian Children," *Child Development* 43 (1972):1104–10.

27. Graves and Graves, "The Cultural Context of Prosocial Development."

28. Rohner, *They Love Me, They Love Me Not*, pp. 129, 130.

29. Ibid., p. 132.

30. Ibid., p. 146.

31. Ibid., p. 148.

32. Mead, *Sex and Temperament in Three Primitive Societies*.

33. E. H. Erikson, *Childhood and Society* (New York: W. W. Norton, 1950); M. D. S. Ainsworth, "Attachment as Related to Mother-Infant Interaction," in *Advances in the Study of Behavior*, vol. 9, ed. J. S. Rosenblatt, R. A. Hinde, C. Beer, and M. Busnel (New York: Academic Press, 1979); R. Kestenbaum, E. A. Farber, and L. A. Sroufe, "Individual Differences in Empathy among Preschoolers: Relation to Attachment History," in *New Directions for Child Development, vol. 44: Empathy and Related Emotional Responses*, ed. N. Eisenberg (San Francisco: Jossey-Bass, 1989).

34. Rohner, *They Love Me, They Love Me Not.*

35. Dennis, *The Hopi Child.*

36. Shapiro and Madsen, "Kibbutz and Urban Children in Israel."

37. U. Bronfenbrenner, *Two Worlds of Childhood: U.S. and U.S.S.R.* (New York: Russell Sage Foundation, 1970), p. 21.

38. Madsen, "Children in Three Mexican Sub-Cultures."

39. Graves and Graves, "The Cultural Context of Prosocial Development," p. 248.

40. J. W. M. Whiting and B. B. Whiting, "Altruistic and Egoistic Behavior in Six Cultures," in *Cultural Illness and Health,* ed. L. Nader and T. Maretzki (Washington, D.C.: American Anthropological Association, 1973); B. B. Whiting and J. W. M. Whiting, *Children of Six Cultures: A Psychocultural Analysis* (Cambridge, Mass.: Harvard University Press, 1975).

41. Whiting and Whiting, *Children of Six Cultures.*

42. Whiting and Whiting, "Altruistic and Egoistic Behavior," p. 64.

43. Ibid.; Graves and Graves, "The Cultural Context of Prosocial Development."

44. Graves and Graves, "Cultural Context of Prosocial Development," p. 248.

7 / SOCIALIZATION IN THE FAMILY

1. S. P. Oliner and P. M. Oliner, *The Altruistic Personality: Rescuers of Jews in Nazi Europe* (New York: Free Press, 1988).

2. Ibid., pp. 164–165.

3. Ibid., p. 165.

4. Ibid., p. 166.

5. Ibid., p. 168.

6. Ibid., p. 180.

7. A. Bandura, "Social-Learning Theory of Identificatory Processes," in *Handbook of Socialization Theory and Research,* ed. D. A. Goslin (Chicago: Rand-McNally, 1969), pp. 213–262; idem, *Social Foundations of Thought and Action: A Social Cognitive Theory* (Englewood Cliffs, N.J.: Prentice-Hall, 1986).

8. Bandura, "Social-Learning Theory of Identificatory Pro-

cesses"; E. Rutherford and P. Mussen, "Generation in Nursery and School Boys," *Child Development* 39 (1968):755–765; L. Kohlberg, "Stage and Sequence: The Cognitive-Developmental Approach to Socialization," in Goslin, *Handbook of Socialization Theory and Research*, pp. 325–480.

9. See B. S. Moore and N. Eisenberg, "The Development of Altruism," in *Annals of Child Development*, ed. G. Whitehurst (Greenwich, Conn.: JAI Press), pp. 107–174; M. Radke-Yarrow, C. Zahn-Waxler, and M. Chapman, "Prosocial Dispositions and Behavior," in *Manual of Child Psychology*, ed. E. M. Hetherington, vol. 4: *Socialization, Personality, and Social Development*, ed. P. Mussen (New York: John Wiley & Sons, 1983), pp. 469–545.

10. C. Zahn-Waxler, M. Radke-Yarrow, and R. A. King, "Child Rearing and Children's Prosocial Initiations toward Victims of Distress," *Child Development* 50 (1979):319–330.

11. Rutherford and Mussen, "Generation in Nursery School Boys."

12. D. L. Rosenhan, "The Natural Socialization of Altruistic Autonomy," in *Altruism and Helping Behavior*, ed. J. Macaulay and L. Berkowitz (New York: Academic Press, 1970), pp. 262–263.

13. P. London, "The Rescuers: Motivational Hypotheses about Christians Who Saved Jews from the Nazis," in Macaulay and Berkowitz, *Altruism and Helping Behavior*, pp. 241–250

14. Rosenhan, "The Natural Socialization of Altruistic Autonomy."

15. E. G. Clary and J. Miller, "Socialization and Situational Influences on Sustained Altruism," *Child Development* 57 (1986):1358–69.

16. C. S. Weissbrod, "Noncontingent Warmth Induction, Cognitive Style, and Children's Imitative Donation and Rescue Effort Behaviors," *Journal of Personality and Social Psychology* 34 (1976):274–281.

17. Clary and Miller, "Socialization and Situational Influences on Sustained Altruism," 1361.

18. J. H. Bryan and N. H. Walbek, "The Impact of Words

and Deeds concerning Altruism upon Children," *Child Development* 41 (1970):747–757; idem, "Preaching and Practicing Generosity: Children's Actions and Reactions," *Child Development* 41 (1970) 329–353.

19. N. Eisenberg-Berg and E. Geisheker, "Content of Preachings and Power of the Model/Preacher: The Effect on Children's Generosity," *Developmental Psychology* 15 (1979):168–175.

20. See Moore and Eisenberg, "The Development of Altruism."

21. Clary and Miller, "Socialization and Situational Influences on Sustained Altruism"; Rosenhan, "The Natural Socialization of Altruistic Autonomy."

22. M. S. Brown and A. C. Israel, "Effects of Instructions, Self-Instructions, and Discipline on Children's Donating" (Paper presented at the annual meeting of the American Psychological Association, Montreal, September 1980); A. C. Israel and M. S. Brown, "Effects of Directiveness of Instructions and Surveillance on the Production and Persistence of Children's Donations," *Journal of Experimental Child Psychology* 27 (1979):250–261; A. C. Israel and P. A. Raskin, "Directiveness of Instructions and Modeling: Effects on Productions and Persistence on Children's Donations," *Journal of Genetic Psychology* 135 (1979):269–277; G. M. White and M. A. Burnam, "Socially Cued Altruism: Effects of Modeling, Instructions, and Age on Public and Private Donations," *Child Development* 46 (1975):559–563.

23. E. J. Barton, "Developing Sharing: An Analysis of Modeling and Other Behavioral Techniques," *Behavior Modification* 5 (1981):386–398; E. J. Barton and F. R. Ascione, "Sharing in Preschool Children: Facilitation, Stimulus Generalization, Response Generalization, and Maintenance," *Journal of Applied Behavioral Analysis* 12 (1979):417–430; N. Eisenberg, R. B. Cialdini, H. McCreath, and R. Shell, "Consistency-Based Compliance: When and Why Do Children Become Vulnerable?" *Journal of Personality and Social Psychology* 52 (1987):1174–81; E. Staub, *Positive Social Behavior and Morality*, vol. 2: *Socialization and Development* (New York: Academic Press, 1979).

24. Eisenberg et al., "Consistency-Based Compliance."

25. J. E. Grusec and E. Redler, "Attribution, Reinforcement, and Altruism: A Developmental Analysis," *Developmental Psychology* 16 (1980):525–534.

26. A. M. Jensen and S. G. Moore, "The Effect of Attribute Statements on Cooperativeness and Competitiveness in School-Age Boys," *Child Development* 48 (1977):305–307: I. J. Toner, L. P. Moore, and B. A. Emmons, "The Effect of Being Labeled on Subsequent Self-Control in Children," *Child Development* 51 (1980):618–621; R. L. Miller, P. Brickman, and D. Bolen, "Attribution versus Persuasion as a Means for Modifing Behavior," *Journal of Personality and Social Psychology* 31 (1975):430–441.

27. J. E. Grusec, "The Socialization of Altruism," in *The Development of Prosocial Behavior*, ed. N. Eisenberg (New York: Academic Press, 1982), pp. 65–90.

28. Moore and Eisenberg, "The Development of Altruism"; Radke-Yarrow, Zahn-Waxler, and Chapman, "Prosocial Dispositions and Behavior."

29. Zahn-Waxler, Radke-Yarrow, and King, "Children's Prosocial Initiations toward Victims of Distress."

30. M. L. Hoffman, "Moral Development," in *Carmichael's Manual of Child Development*, vol. 2, ed. P. H. Mussen (New York: John Wiley & Sons, 1970), pp. 261–359; idem, "Altruistic Behavior and the Parent-Child Relationship," *Journal of Personality and Social Psychology* 31 (1975):937–943.

31. M. L. Hoffman, "Parent Discipline and the Child's Consideration for Others," *Child Development* 34 (1963):573–588.

32. E. L. Dlugokinski and I. J. Firestone, "Other Centeredness and Susceptibility to Charitable Appeals: Effects of Perceived Discipline," *Developmental Psychology* 10 (1974):21–28.

33. Hoffman, "Moral Development"; Staub, *Socialization and Development*.

34. Moore and Eisenberg, "The Development of Altruism"; Radke-Yarrow, Zahn-Waxler, and Chapman, "Prosocial Dispositions and Behavior."

35. Hoffman, "Parent Discipline and the Child's Consideration for Others."

36. D. Baumrind, "Current Patterns of Parental Author-ity," *Developmental Psychology Mongraphs* 4 (1971):1–103.

37. Hoffman, "Moral Development"; Staub, *Socialization and Development*.

38. D. P. Hartmann, C. C. Cromer, C. L. Smith, and B. C. Page, "The Effects of Instructional Prompts and Praise on Children's Donation Rates," *Child Development* 44 (1975):980–983; see Moore and Eisenberg, "The Development of Altruism."

39. Barton, "Developing Sharing"; A. Rogers-Warren and D. M. Baer, "Correspondence between Saying and Doing: Teaching Children to Share and Praise," *Journal of Applied Behavioral Analysis* 9 (1976):335–354.

40. J. E. Grusec, "The Internalization of Altruistic Disposi-tions: A Cognitive Analysis," in *Social Cognition and Social Development: A Sociocultural Perspective,* ed. E. T. Higgins, D. N. Ruble, and W. W. Hartup (Cambridge: Cambridge University Press, 1983), pp. 275–293; M. R. Lepper, "Social-Control Processes and the Internalization of Social Values: An Attributional Perspective," ibid., pp. 294–330.

41. R. A. Fabes, J. Fultz, N. Eisenberg, T. May-Plumlee, and F. S. Christopher, "The Effects of Reward on Children's Prosocial Motivation: A Socialization Study," *Developmental Psychology* 25 (1989):509–515.

42. Baumrind, "Current Patterns of Parental Authority"; see Moore and Eisenberg, "The Development of Altruism."

43. Hoffman, "Moral Development."

44. M. D. S. Ainsworth, "Attachment as Related to Mother–Infant Interaction," in *Advances in the Study of Behavior*, vol. 9, ed. J. S. Rosenblatt, R. A. Hinde, C. Beer, and M. Busnel (New York: Academic Press, 1979), pp. 2–51.

45. E. Waters, J. Wippmann, and L. A. Sroufe, "Attach-ment, Positive Affect, and Competence in the Peer Group: Two Studies in Construct Validation," *Child Development* 50 (1979):821–829.

46. R. Kestenbaum, E. A. Farber, and L. A. Sroufe, "Indi-vidual Differences in Empathy among Preschoolers: Relation to Attachment History," in *New Directions for Child Develop-*

ment, vol. 44: *Empathy and Related Emotional Responses*, ed. N. Eisenberg (San Francisco: Jossey-Bass, 1989), pp. 51–64.

47. N. D. Feshbach, "Sex Differences in Empathy and Social Behavior in Children," in Eisenberg, *The Development of Prosocial Behavior*, pp. 315–338; S. Feshbach and N. D. Feshbach, "Aggression and Altruism: A Personality Perspective," in *Altruism and Aggression: Biological and Social Origins*, ed. C. Zahn-Waxler, E. M. Cummings, and R. Iannotti (Cambridge: Cambridge University Press, 1986), pp. 189–217.

48. Feshbach and Feshbach, "Aggression and Altruism"; Hoffman, "Moral Development"; M. B. Shure, "Interpersonal Problem Solving: A Cog in the Wheel of Social Cognition," in *Social-Cognitive Development in Context*, ed. F. C. Serafica (New York: Guildford Press, 1982), pp. 133–166.

49. M. Schulman and E. Mekler, *Bringing Up a Moral Child* (Reading, Mass.: Addison-Wesley, 1985), p. 67.

50. S. Bank and M. D. Kahn, "Sisterhood-Brotherhood Is Powerful: Sibling Subsystems and Family Therapy," *Family Process* 14 (1975):311–337.

51. M. E. Lamb, "Sibling Relationships across the Lifespan," in *Sibling Relationships*, ed. M. E. Lamb and B. Sutton-Smith (Hillsdale, N.J.: Erlbaum and Associates, 1982), p. 6.

52. J. Dunn, "Sibling Relationships in Early Childhood," *Child Development* 54 (1983):787–811; D. Pepler, C. Corter, and R. Abramovitch, "Social Relations among Children: Comparison of Siblings and Peer Interaction," in *Peer Relationships and Social Skills in Childhood*, ed. K. Rubin and H. S. Ross (New York: Springer-Verlag, 1982), pp. 209–227.

53. J. Dunn, *The Beginnings of Social Understanding* (Cambridge, Mass.: Harvard University Press, 1988), p. 91.

54. Dunn, *The Beginnings of Social Understanding*.

55. J. Dunn and C. Kendrick, *Siblings: Love, Envy, and Understanding* (Cambridge, Mass.: Harvard University Press, 1982), p. 115.

56. J. Dunn, *Sisters and Brothers* (Cambridge, Mass.: Harvard University Press, 1983), p. 16.

57. Ibid.

58. J. Dunn and P. Munn, "Siblings and the Development of Prosocial Behavior," *International Journal of Behavioral Development* 9 (1986):265–284; M. Summers, "Imitation, Dominance, Agonism, and Prosocial Behavior: A Meta-Analysis of Sibling Behavior" (Paper presented at the biennial meeting of the Society for Research in Child Development, Baltimore, April 1987).

59. Summers, "Imitation, Dominance, Agonism, and Prosocial Behavior."

60. P. W. Berman, "Are Women More Responsive than Men to the Young? A Review of Developmental and Situational Variables," *Psychological Bulletin* 88 (1980):668–695; idem, "Children Caring for Babies: Age and Sex Differences in Response to Infant Signals and to the Social Context," in *Contemporary Topics on Developmental Psychology*, ed. N. Eisenberg (New York: Wiley, 1987), pp. 141–164.

61. Dunn and Munn, "Siblings and the Development of Prosocial Behavior."

62. B. K. Bryant and S. B. Crockenberg, "Correlates and Dimensions of Prosocial Behavior: A Study of Female Siblings with Their Mothers," *Child Development* 51 (1980):529–544.

63. Ibid., p. 538.

64. J. Dunn and C. Kendrick, "Siblings and Their Mothers: Developing Relationships within the Family," in Lamb and Sutton-Smith, *Sibling Relationships*, pp. 39–60.

65. G. H. Brody, Z. Stoneman, and C. E. MacKinnon, "Contributions of Maternal Child-Rearing Practices and Play Contexts to Sibling Interactions," *Journal of Applied Developmental Psychology* 7 (1986):225–236.

66. Kestenbaum, Farber, and Sroufe, "Individual Differences in Empathy among Preschoolers."

8 / SOCIALIZATION OUTSIDE THE HOME

1. W. W. Hartup, "Peer Relations," in *Handbook of Child Development*, ed. E. M. Hetherington, vol. 4: *Socialization Personality and Social Development*, ed. P. H. Mussen (New York: John Wiley & Sons, 1983), pp. 103–196.

2. J. Youniss and J. Smollar, *Adolescent Relations with Mothers, Fathers, and Friends* (Chicago: University of Chicago Press, 1985).

3. M. R. Yarrow, P. M. Scott, and C. Z. Waxler, "Learning Concern for Others," *Developmental Psychology* 8 (1973):240–260.

4. N. Eisenberg-Berg and E. Geisheker, "Content of Preachings and Power of the Model/Preacher: The Effect on Children's Generosity," *Developmental Psychology* 15 (1979):168–175.

5. N. Eisenberg and P. H. Mussen, *The Roots of Prosocial Behavior in Children* (Cambridge: Cambridge University Press, 1989).

6. U. Bronfenbrenner, *Two Worlds of Childhood: U.S. and U.S.S.R.* (New York: Russell Sage Foundation, 1970).

7. N. D. Feshbach, "Sex Differences in Empathy and Social Behavior in Children," in *The Development of Prosocial Behavior*, ed. N. Eisenberg (New York: Academic Press, 1982), pp. 315–338; S. Feshbach and N. D. Feshbach, "Aggression and Altruism: A Personality Perspective," in *Altruism and Aggression: Biological and Social Origins*, ed. C. Zahn-Waxler, E. M. Cummings, and R. Iannotti (Cambridge: Cambridge University Press, 1986), pp. 189–217.

8. N. D. Feshbach, S. Feshbach, M. Fauvre, and M. Ballard-Campbell, *Learning to Care: Classroom Activities for Social and Affective Development* (Glenview, Ill.: Scott, Foresman, 1983), p. 24.

9. Ibid., p. 66.

10. Ibid., p. 24.

11. Ibid., p. 18.

12. Feshbach, "Sex Differences in Empathy and Social Behavior"; Feshbach and Feshbach, "Aggression and Altruism"; Feshbach et al., p. 24.

13. S. Sharan, P. Hare, C. D. Webb, and R. Hertz-Lazarowitz, *Cooperation in Education* (Provo: Brigham Young University Press, 1980).

14. R. Hertz-Lazarowitz and S. Sharan, "Enhancing Prosocial Behavior through Cooperative Learning in the Class-

room," in *Development and Maintenance of Prosocial Behavior: International Perspectives on Positive Behavior*, ed. E. Staub, D. Bar-Tal, J. Karylowski, and J. Reykowski (New York: Plenum Press, 1984), pp. 429.

15. E. Aronson, N. Blaney, C. Stephan, J. Sikes, and M. Snapp, *The Jigsaw Classroom* (Beverly Hills: Sage, 1978).

16. N. T. Blaney, C. Stephan, D. Rosenfield, E. Aronson, and J. Sikes, "Interdependence in the Classroom: A Field Study," *Journal of Educational Psychology* 69 (1977):139–176.

17. K. Savesky and V. Malcarne, *People and Animals: A Humane Education Curriculum Guide* (East Haddam, Conn.: National Association for the Advancement of Humane Education, 1981), p. iii.

18. F. R. Ascione, "Enhancing Children's Attitudes about the Humane Treatment of Animals: Generalization to Human-Directed Empathy" (Paper presented at the biennial meeting of the Society for Research in Child Development, Seattle, April 1991).

19. V. Battistich, M. Watson, D. Solomon, and E. Schaps, "The Child Development Project: A Comprehensive Program for the Development of Prosocial Character," in *Moral Behavior and Development*, vol. 1: *Advances in Theory, Research, and Application*, ed. W. M. Kurtines and J. L. Gewirtz (Hillsdale, N.J.: Lawrence Erlbaum Associates, in press), p. 2.

20. D. Solomon, M. S. Watson, K. L. Delucchi, E. Schaps, and V. Battistich, "Enhancing Children's Prosocial Behavior in the Classroom," *American Educational Research Journal* 25 (1988): 531.

21. T. J. Berndt, "The Distinctive Features of Conversations between Friends: Theories, Research, and Implications for Sociomoral Development," in *Moral Development through Social Interaction*, ed. W. M. Kurtines and J. L. Gewirtz (New York: John Wiley & Sons, 1987), pp. 281–300; Youniss and Smollar, *Adolescent Relations with Mothers, Fathers, and Friends*.

22. Youniss and Smollar, *Adolescent Relations with Mothers, Fathers, and Friends*, p. 94.

23. Hartup, "Peer Relations"; R. L. Selman, *The Growth of Interpersonal Understanding: Developmental and Clinical Analysis* (New York: Academic Press, 1980).

24. N. Eisenberg, K. Tryon, and E. Cameron, "The Relationship of Preschoolers' Peer Interaction to Their Sex-Typed Toy Choices," *Child Development* 55 (1984):1044–50; R. Shell and N. Eisenberg, "The Role of Peer Interaction in Gender-Typed Toy Play," *Journal of Behavioral Development* 13 (1990):373–388; B. I. Fagot, "Consequences of Moderate Cross-Gender Behavior in Preschool Children," *Child Development* 48 (1977):902–907.

25. G. R. Patterson, R. A. Littman, and W. Bricker, "Assertive Behavior in Children: A Step toward a Theory of Aggression," *Monographs of the Society for Research in Child Development* 32 (1967):5, serial no. 113.

26. A. Bandura, *Aggression: A Social Learning Analysis* (Englewood Cliffs, N.J.: Prentice-Hall, 1973); K. Bussey and D. G. Perry, "The Imitation of Resistance to Deviation: Conclusive Evidence for an Elusive Effect," *Developmental Psychology* 13 (1977):438–443; R. O'Connor, "Modification of Social Withdrawal through Symbolic Modeling," *Journal of Applied Behavior Analysis* 2 (1969):15–22; see G. H. Brody and D. R. Shaffer, "Contributions of Parents and Peers to Children's Moral Socialization," *Developmental Review* 2 (1982):31–75.

27. Z. Stoneman and G. H. Brody, "Peers as Mediators of Television Food Advertisements Aimed at Children," *Developmental Psychology* 17 (1981):853–858.

28. W. W. Hartup and B. Coates, "Imitation of a Peer as a Function of Reinforcement from the Peer Group and Rewardingness of the Model," *Child Development* 38 (1967):1003–16; R. Elliott and R. Vasta, "The Modeling of Sharing: Effects Associated with Vicarious Reinforcement, Symbolization, Age, and Generalization," *Journal of Experimental Child Psychology* 10 (1970):8–15; P. S. Strain, T. P. Cooke, and T. Apollini, "The Role of Peers in Modifying Classmates' Social Behavior: A Review," *Journal of Special Education* 10 (1976):351–356.

29. F. R. Ascione and R. L. Sanok, "The Role of Peer and Adult Models in Facilitating and Inhibiting Children's Prosocial Behavior," *Genetic Psychology Monographs* 106 (1982):239–259.

30. R. G. Wahler, "Child-Child Interactions in Five Field

Settings: Some Experimental Evidence," *Journal of Experimental Child Psychology* 5 (1967):278–293.

31. N. Eisenberg, E. Cameron, K. Tryon, and R. Dodez, "Socialization of Prosocial Behavior in the Preschool Classroom," *Developmental Psychology* 17 (1981):773–782.

32. W. Furman, D. F. Rahe, and W. W. Hartup, "Rehabilitation of Socially Withdrawn Preschool Children through Mixed-Age and Same-Age Socialization," *Child Development* 50 (1979):915–922.

33. J. Piaget, *The Moral Judgment of the Child* (1932; reprint, New York: Free Press, 1965); J. Youniss, *Parents and Peers in Social Development: A Sullivan-Piaget Perspective* (Chicago: University of Chicago Press, 1980).

34. Youniss, *Parents and Peers in Social Development*, pp. 74–77.

35. Ibid., pp. 65–69.

36. Ibid.

37. N. Eisenberg, N. Lundy, R. Shell, and K. Roth, "Children's Justifications for Their Adult and Peer-Directed Compliant (Prosocial and Nonprosocial) Behaviors," *Developmental Psychology* 21 (1985):325–331.

38. Ibid.

39. J. P. Rushton, *Altruism, Socialization, and Society* (Englewood Cliffs, N.J.: Prentice-Hall, 1980); J. P. Rushton, "Television as a Socializer," in *Altruism and Helping Behavior*, ed. J. P. Rushton and R. M. Sorrentino (Hillsdale, N.J.: Erlbaum and Associates 1981).

40. J. P. Rushton, *Altruism, Socialization, and Society* (Englewood Cliffs, N.J.: Prentice-Hall, 1980), p. 135.

41. Rushton, *Altruism, Socialization, and Society*.

42. Ibid.

43. L. K. Friedrich-Cofer and A. C. Huston, "Television Violence and Aggression: The Debate Continues," *Psychological Bulletin* 100 (1986):364–371; National Institute of Mental Health, *Television and Behavior*, vol. 1 (Washington, D.C.: U.S. Government Printing Office, 1982).

44. L. D. Eron, "The Development of Aggressive Behavior from the Perspective of a Developing Behaviorism," *American*

Psychologist 42 (1987):435–442; L. D. Eron, M. M. Lefkowitz, L. R. Huesmann, and L. O. Walder, "Does Television Violence Cause Aggression? *American Psychologist* 27 (1972):253–263.

45. Friedrich-Cofer and Huston, "Television Violence and Aggression."

46. W. A. Collins and S. K. Getz, "Children's Social Responses Following Modeled Reactions to Provocation: Prosocial Effects of a Television Drama," *Journal of Personality* 44 (1976):488–500.

47. J. M. Sprafkin, R. M. Liebert, and R. W. Poulos, "Effects of a Prosocial Example on Children's Helping," *Journal of Experimental Child Psychology* 20 (1975):119–126.

48. L. K. Friedrich and A. H. Stein, "Aggressive and Prosocial Television Programs and the Natural Behavior of Preschool Children," *Monographs of the Society for Research in Child Development* 38 (1973):4, serial no. 151.

49. I. M. Ahammer and J. P. Murray, "Kindness in the Kindergarten: The Relative Influence of Role Playing and Prosocial Television in Facilitating Altruism," *International Journal of Behavioral Development* 2 (1979):133–157; Friedrich-Cofer and Huston, "Television Violence and Aggression."

50. Rushton, "Television as a Socializer."

9 / THE EFFECT OF CIRCUMSTANCES

1. D. Magnusson and N. S. Endler, *Personality at the Crossroads: Current Issues in Interactional Psychology* (Hillsdale, N.J.: Lawrence Erlbaum Associates, 1977); W. Mischel, "Continuity and Change in Personality," *American Psychologist* 24 (1969):1012–18; D. Romer, C. L. Gruder, and T. Lizzardo, "A Person-Situation Approach to Altruistic Behavior," *Journal of Personality and Social Psychology* 51 (1986):1001–12.

2. S. P. Oliner and P. M. Oliner, *The Altruistic Personality: Rescuers of Jews in Nazi Europe* (New York: Free Press, 1988), p. 131.

3. P. Hallie, *Lest Innocent Blood Be Shed: The Story of the*

Chambon and How Goodness Happened There (New York: Harper & Row, 1979).

4. R. B. Cialdini, D. J. Baumann, and D. T. Kenrick, "Insights from Sadness: A Three-Step Model of the Development of Altruism as Hedonism," *Developmental Review* 1 (1981):207–223; D. L. Rosenhan, P. Salovey, J. Karylowski, and K. Hargis, "Emotion and Altruism," in *Altruism and Helping Behavior: Social, Personality, and Developmental Perspectives,* ed. J. P. Rushton and R. M. Sorrentino (Hillsdale, N.J.: Lawrence Erlbaum Associates, 1981), pp. 233–248.

5. A. M. Isen, M. Clark, and M. F. Schwartz, "Duration of the Effect of Mood on Helping: "Footprints in the Sands of Time," *Journal of Personality and Social Psychology* 34 (1976):385–393.

6. J. M. McGuire and M. H. Thomas, "Effects of Sex, Competence, and Competition on Sharing Behavior in Children," *Journal of Personality and Social Psychology* 32 (1975):490–494.

7. R. B. Cialdini, D. T. Kenrick, and D. J. Baumann, "Effects of Mood on Prosocial Behavior in Children and Adults," in *The Development of Prosocial Behavior,* ed. N. Eisenberg (New York: Academic Press, 1982), pp. 339–359; D. R. Shaffer, "Is Mood-Induced Altruism a Form of Hedonism?" *Humboldt Journal of Social Relations* 13 (1986):195–216.

8. A. M. Isen, T. E. Shalker, M. Clark, and L. Karp, "Affect, Accessibility of Material in Memory, and Behavior: A Cognitive Loop?" *Journal of Personality and Social Psychology* 36 (1978):1–12.

9. Cialdini, Kenrick, and Baumann, "Effects of Mood on Prosocial Behavior."

10. A. M. Isen, N. Horn, and D. L. Rosenhan, "Effects of Success and Failure on Children's Generosity," *Journal of Personality and Social Psychology* 27 (1973):239–247.

11. Cialdini, Kenrick, and Baumann, "Effects of Mood on Prosocial Behavior," J. F. Dovidio, "Helping Behavior and Altruism: An Empirical and Conceptual Overview," in *Advances in Experimental Social Psychology,* vol. 17, ed. L. Berkowitz (New York: Academic Press, 1984), pp. 361–427.

12. Cialdini, Kenrick, Baumann, "Effects of Mood on Prosocial Behavior."

13. M. Carlson and N. Miller, "Explanation of the Relation between Negative Mood and Helping," *Psychological Bulletin* 102 (1987):91–108; R. B. Cialdini and D. T. Kenrick, "Altruism as Hedonism: A Social Development Perspective on the Relationship of Negative Mood State and Helping," *Journal of Personality and Social Psychology* 34 (1976):907–914.

14. M. A. Barnett, L. M. King, and J. A. Howard, "Inducing Affect about Self or Other: Effects on Generosity in Children," *Developmental Psychology* 15 (1979):164–167; Rosenham et al., "Emotion and Altruism."

15. Dovidio, "Helping Behavior and Altruism."

16. B. J. Mosbacher, G. E. Gruen, and J. F. Rychlak, "Incentive Value: The Overlooked Dimension in Childhood Sharing," *Journal of Genetic Psychology* 146 (1985):197–204.

17. N. Eisenberg and R. Fabes, unpublished data (1989).

18. G. W. Ladd, G. Lange, and A. Stremmel, "Personal and Situational Influences on Children's Helping Behavior: Factors That Mediate Compliant Helping," *Child Development* 54 (1983):488–501; O. Zinser and E. W. Lydiatt, "Mode of Recipient Definitions, Affluence of the Recipient, and Sharing Behavior in Preschool Children," *Journal of Genetic Psychology* 129 (1976):261–266; O. Zinser, J. S. Perry, and R. M. Edgar, "Affluence of the Recipient, Value of Donations, and Sharing Behavior in Preschool Children," *Journal of Psychology* 89 (1975):301–305.

19. Dovidio, "Helping Behavior and Altruism."

20. G. T. Fouts, "Charity in Children: The Influence of 'Charity' Stimuli and an Audience," *Journal of Experimental Child Psychology* 13 (1972):303–309; Zinser and Lydiatt, "Mode of Recipient Definitions and Sharing Behavior"; Zinser, Perry, and Edgar, "Affluence of the Recipient and Sharing Behavior."

21. R. M. Liebert, L. E. Fernandez, and L. Gill, "Effects of a 'Friendless' Model on Imitation and Prosocial Behavior," *Psychonomic Science* 16 (1969):81–82.

22. M. E. Lamb, "Interactions between Eighteen-Month-Olds and Their Preschool-Aged Siblings," *Child Development* 49 (1978):51–59; idem, "The Development of Sibling Relationships in Infancy: A Short-Term Longitudinal Study," *Child*

Development 49 (1978):1189–96; H. L. Rheingold, D. F. Hay, and M. J. West, "Sharing in the Second Year of Life," *Child Development* 47 (1976):1148–58.

23. Dovidio, "Helping Behavior and Altruism"; A. D. Panofsky, "The Effect of Similarity/Dissimilarity of Race and Personal Interests on Empathy and Altruism in Second Graders," *Dissertation Abstracts International* 37 (1976):200A (Ph.D. diss., University of California, Los Angeles); J. B. Willis, N. S. Feldman, and D. N. Ruble, "Children's Generosity as Influenced by Deservedness of Reward and Type of Recipient," *Journal of Educational Psychology* 69 (1977):33–35.

24. N. Eisenberg, "Children's Differentiations among Potential Recipients of Aid," *Child Development* 54 (1983):594–602.

25. Ibid.; M. L. Hoffman, "Interaction of Affect and Cognition in Empathy," in *Emotions, Cognitions, and Behavior,* ed. C. E. Izard, J. Kagan, and R. B. Zajonc (Cambridge: Cambridge University Press, 1984), pp. 103–131.

26. F. Crosby, S. Bromely, and L. Saxe, "Recent Unobstrusive Studies of Black and White Discrimination and Prejudice: A Literature Review," *Psychological Bulletin* 87 (1980):546–563; D. L. Frey and S. L. Gaertner, "Helping and the Avoidance of Inappropriate Interracial Behavior: A Strategy That Perpetuates a Nonprejudiced Self-Image," *Journal of Personality and Social Psychology* 50 (1986):1083–90; J. A. Piliavin, J. F. Dovidio, S. L. Gaertner, and R. D. Clark III, *Emergency Intervention* (New York: Academic Press, 1981).

27. P. A. Katz, I. Katz, and S. Cohen, "White Children's Attitudes toward Blacks and the Physically Handicapped: A Developmental Study," *Journal of Educational Psychology* 82 (1976):20–24; Panofsky, "Similarity/Dissimilarity of Race and Personal Interests"; O. Zinser, J. S. Perry, R. G. Bailey, and E. W. Lydiatt, "Racial Recipients, Value of Donations, and Sharing Behavior in Children," *Journal of Genetic Psychology* 129 (1976):29–35; Eisenberg, "Children's Differentiations among Potential Recipients of Aid."

28. H. Bengtsson and L. Johnson, "Cognitions Related to Empathy in 5-to-11-Year-Old Children," *Child Development* 58

(1987):1001–12; N. D. Feshbach, "Studies of Empathic Behavior in Children," in *Progress in Experimental Personality Research*, vol. 8, ed. B. A. Maher (New York: Academic Press, 1978), pp. 1–47.

29. E. Staub and H. Noerenberg, "Property Rights, Deservingness, Reciprocity, Friendship: The Transactional Character of Children's Sharing Behavior," *Journal of Personality and Social Psychology* 40 (1981):271–289; see T. J. Berndt, "The Distinctive Features of Conversations between Friends: Theories, Research, and Implications for Sociomoral Development," in *Moral Development through Social Interaction*, ed. W. M. Kurtines and J. L. Gewirtz (New York: John Wiley & Sons, 1987), pp. 281–300; N. Eisenberg and J. F. Pasternack, "Inequities in Children's Prosocial Behavior: Whom Do Children Assist?" in *The Child's Construction of Social Inequity*, ed. R. L. Leahy (New York: Academic Press, 1983), pp. 179–205.

30. Berndt, "The Distinctive Features of Conversations between Friends."

31. M. S. Clark, "Noncomparability of Benefits Given and Received: A Cue to the Existence of Friendship," *Social Psychology Quarterly* 44 (1981):375–381; E. Staub and L. Sherk, "Need for Approval, Children's Sharing Behavior, and Reciprocity in Sharing," *Child Development* 41 (1970):243–252.

32. R. Charlesworth and W. W. Hartup, "Positive Social Reinforcement in the Nursery School Peer Group," *Child Development* 38 (1967):993–1002; N. Eisenberg-Berg and M. Hand, "The Relationship of Preschoolers' Reasoning about Prosocial Moral Conflicts to Prosocial Behavior," *Child Development* 50 (1979):356–363; R. F. Marcus and B. Jenny, "A Naturalistic Study of Reciprocity in the Helping Behavior of Young Children," *Alberta Journal of Educational Research* 23 (1977):195–206.

33. Ladd, Lange, and Stremmel, "Personal and Situational Influences on Children's Helping Behavior"; J. Walters, D. Pearce, and L. Dahms, "Affectional and Aggressive Behavior of Preschool Children," *Child Development* 28 (1957):15–26.

34. A. H. Eagly and M. Crowley, "Gender and Helping Behavior: A Meta-Analytic Review of the Social Psychological

186 / Notes to Page 139

Literature," *Psychological Bulletin* 100 (1986):283–308; R. S. Zeldin, S. A. Small, and R. C. Savin-Williams, "Prosocial Interactions in Two Mixed-Sex Adolescent Groups," *Child Development* 53 (1982):1492–98.

35. J. Gottman, J. Gonso, and B. Rasmussen, "Social Interaction, Social Competence, and Friendship in Children," *Child Development* 46 (1975):709–718; J. C. Masters and W. Furnam, "Popularity, Individual Friendship Selection, and Specific Peer Interaction among Children," *Developmental Psychology* 17 (1981):344–350; A. Raviv, D. Bar-Tal, H. Ayalon, and A. Ravir, "Perception of Giving and Receiving Help by Group Members," *Representative Research in Social Psychology* 11 (1980):140–151.

36. L. Furby, "Sharing: Decisions and Moral Judgments about Letting Others Use One's Possessions," *Psychological Reports* 43 (1978):595–609; J. J. Leung and S. F. Foster, "Helping the Elderly: A Study on Altruism in Children," *Child Study Journal* 15 (1985):293–309.

37. Marcus and Jenny, "A Naturalistic Study of Reciprocity"; E. Staub and H. K. Feinberg, "Regularities in Peer Interaction, Empathy, and Sensitivity to Others" (Paper presented at the annual meeting of the American Psychological Association, Montreal, September 1980).

38. L. Berkowitz and P. Friedman, "Same Social Class Differences in Helping Behavior," *Journal of Personality and Social Psychology* 5 (1967):217–225; S. B. Dreman, "Sharing Behavior in Israeli School Children: Cognitive and Social Learning Factors," *Child Development* 47 (1976):186–194; S. B. Dreman and C. W. Greenbaum, "Altruism or Reciprocity: Sharing Behavior in Israeli Kindergarten Children," *Child Development* 44 (1973):61–68; Staub and Sherk, "Need for Approval and Reciprocity in Sharing."

39. C. P. Baldwin and A. L. Baldwin, "Children's Judgments of Kindness," *Child Development* 41 (1970):29–47; L. Peterson, D. P. Hartmann, and D. M. Gelfand, "Developmental Changes in the Effects of Dependency and Reciprocity Cues on Children's Moral Judgments and Donation Rates," *Child Development* 48 (1977):1331–39; J. Suls, S. Witenberg,

and D. Gutkin, "Evaluating Reciprocal and Nonreciprocal Prosocial Behavior: Developmental Changes," *Personality and Social Psychology Bulletin* 7 (1981):25–31.

40. L. Furby, "Sharing"; L. Peterson, "Developmental Changes in Verbal and Behavioral Sensitivity to Cues of Social Norms of Altruism," *Child Development* 51 (1980):830–838.

41. M. A. Barnett, "Effects of Competition and Relative Deservedness of the Other's Fate on Children's Generosity," *Developmental Psychology* 11 (1975):665–666; J. Braband and M. J. Lerner, "A Little Time and Effort . . . Who Deserves What from Whom," *Personality and Social Psychology Bulletin* 1 (1975):177–179; see N. Eisenberg, *Altruistic Emotion, Cognition, and Behavior* (Hillsdale, N.J.: Lawrence Erlbaum Associates, 1986); B. Weiner, *An Attributional Theory of Motivation and Emotion* (New York: Springer-Verlag, 1986).

42. D. T. Miller and J. Smith, "The Effect of Own Deservingness and Deservingness of Others on Children's Helping Behavior," *Child Development* 48 (1977):617–620.

43. Ladd, Lange, and Stremmel, "Personal and Situational Influences on Children's Helping Behavior."

44. B. Latane and S. Nida, "Ten Years of Research on Group Size and Helping," *Psychological Bulletin* 89 (1981):308–324.

45. E. Midlarksy and M. E. Hannah, "Competence, Reticence, and Helping by Children and Adolescents," *Developmental Psychology* 21 (1985):534–541; L. Peterson, "Role of Donor Competence, Donor Age, and Peer Presence on Helping in an Emergency," *Developmental Psychology* 19 (1983):873–880; E. Staub, "A Child in Distress: The Influence of Age and Number of Witnesses on Children's Attempts to Help," *Journal of Personality and Social Psychology* 14 (1970):130–140.

46. Staub, "A Child in Distress"; Midlarsky and Hannah, "Competence, Reticence, and Helping."

47. Peterson, "Donor Competence, Donor Age, and Peer Presence."

48. E. Staub, "A Child in Distress: The Effects of Focusing Responsibility on Children on Their Attempts to Help," *Developmental Psychology* 2 (1970):152–153; G. Maruyama, S. C.

Fraser, and N. Miller, "Personal Responsibility and Altruism in Children," *Journal of Personality and Social Psychology* 42 (1982):658–664.

49. W. Suda and G. Fouts, "Effects of Peer Presence on Helping in Introverted and Extroverted Children," *Child Development* 51 (1980):1272–275.

10 / CONCLUSIONS

1. See N. Eisenberg, *Altruistic Emotion, Cognition, and Behavior* (Hillsdale, N.J.: Lawrence Erlbaum Associates, 1986), for more detail.

2. S. P. Oliner and P. M. Oliner, *The Altruistic Personality: Rescuers of Jews in Nazi Europe* (New York: Free Press, 1988).

Index